why
bother
with
church?

why bother with church?

the struggle to belong

Simon Jones

Inter-Varsity Press

INTER-VARSITY PRESS
38 De Montfort Street, Leicester LE1 7GP, England
Email: ivp@uccf.org.uk
Website: www.ivpbooks.com

First published 1998 under the title *Struggling to Belong*. Revised and
expanded edition published 2001 under the title *Why Bother with Church?*

British Library Cataloguing in Publication Data
A catalogue record for this book is available from the British Library.

ISBN 0–85111–254–4

Set in Bembo
Typeset in Great Britain by Avocet Typeset, Brill, Aylesbury, Bucks
Printed in Great Britain by Omnia Books Ltd, Glasgow

Inter-Varsity Press is the publishing division of the Universities and Colleges
Christian Fellowship (formerly the Inter-Varsity Fellowship), a student movement
linking Christian Unions in universities and colleges throughout Great Britain,
and a member movement of the International Fellowship of Evangelical Students.
For information about local and national activities write to UCCF, 38 De
Montfort Street, Leicester LE1 7GP, email us at email@uccf.org.uk, or visit the
UCCF website at www.uccf.org.uk.

CONTENTS

Foreword

This book is a manifesto of hope. In a time when the prospects for the Christian church in the West are not promising, Simon Jones has issued a summons to perseverance and optimism. He addresses those people who are weary and almost at the point of resignation, helping them to see beyond the obvious disappointments and inadequacies of church life. Instead of adding to a chorus of disapproval, he helpfully redraws the connections between Jesus Christ, the kingdom of God, and the community of disciples. In so doing he presages a new era in which the church might yet become what it has in its heart to be.

But this is not another in the continuing stream of falsely pragmatic books that offer one more programme as the coming salvation of the church. Like all true Christian hope, this offering is earthed in both the realities of human suffering and the complexities of ecclesiastical life. It is because the author has experienced both these things himself, and understood what it means to be ready to give up, that his call is capable of engaging those of us who have been hurt and disillusioned in our journeys of faith. Simon Jones speaks as an insider and a fellow-traveller.

Let us not underestimate the problems the church faces.

Not only is it failing to win converts in western society; it is losing its own members at an alarming rate. Even more disturbing, perhaps, is the failure of the community of Christ to engage the imaginations and aspirations of the population at large. Instead of being regarded as a vehicle of hope and liberation, the church is frequently seen as a tired organization that promotes outworn ideas through hierarchical control and the imposition of dogma. Those of us involved in the enterprise know that these accusations are both true and untrue.

We long for more. We know the gospel to be good news, even if its vehicle is often flawed and corrupt. That is why this book is so timely, in reminding us why we bother with the whole enterprise at all. Simon Jones uses a combination of biblical insight, imaginative metaphor and practical experience to bring us back to understanding what the purpose of the church is. His is the voice of the compassionate prophet, reminding us of the bigger picture of God's story of involvement with humanity. It is only when we regain the wider vision that we find the energy unleashed to work for change.

The book is carefully earthed in everyday experience. In the host of characters from Simon Jones's own church involvement, you will find yourself. The insights drawn from such encounters and conversations are at once astute, tragic and humorous. It is people, after all, who make up the substance of church life – with all their idiosyncrasies and ambiguities. And it is among such characters that the task of nurturing and encouraging the people of God must take place. Because it is located clearly within the ordinary stuff of church life, this book is full of realistic hope for both clergy and laity.

I do not think it merely affirms getting on with things they way they are, however. Rather it recalls us to the fundamentals of the corporate following of Christ. Given the current situation, Simon Jones is aware that this entails substantial renewal and reformation of the institutional face of the church. He pays attention to the signs of hope that are already in existence, and uses them to inspire us all to the difficult journey which lies ahead of us. The frank conclusion asks whether the future will have a church. The answer to that question will in part be provided by the readers; but they will be far better prepared for the task through this thoughtful and incisive reflection.

Mike Riddell

Preface

Writing a book is a solitary exercise. I have spent hours shut away, typing, deleting and typing some more, occasionally aware of normal life going on in the house around me. But the ideas in the book are not all mine. They were born in conversations and arguments with people and with other authors through their writing. They have been thrashed out as I have struggled as both a church member and a minister, a conference speaker and travelling mission enabler to under-stand what the church is, what it's for, and how I can help it to live up to its calling.

I'm grateful to many who have contributed to my thinking and ideas over the years. I can single out only a few. First, the members of the church in South London that I pastored for seven years taught me immeasurably more than I taught them. With them I am learning what it means to live in community, to support one another, to learn from one another and to discover together just a little of what God has up his sleeve for his church, if only we'll listen to what he's saying and then wrestle together with how we can put it into action. Not that this church is perfect or in any way unique. If I seem to speak with unseemly enthusiasm about it, it is because I love its people dearly and have found it to be a place of calm and support in a stormy world. In short, it's my family.

Secondly, Stephanie Heald, my editor at IVP. She has not given me an easy time. She has demanded that I think about what I'm writing and that I don't slip into giving easy answers or ducking difficult issues and questions. But all through the process she has been tremendously supportive. An author could not ask for more from an editor.

Thirdly, Graham, my surfing chum, and Rhiannon – who has condescended to help an old man understand how young people think and feel about the church – and Eddie and Dallas (good friends and partners from my church) have all read the whole manuscript, and have commented on it graciously and constructively. It would be a much worse book without their input.

Fourthly, Darrell Jackson has helpfully commented on statistics and loads of other things.

Finally, Linda, Charlie and Olivia have given me the space I needed to write. But far more than that, they have modelled community to me through their support, admonition, humour, love and hugs. And authors need lots of hugs.

Simon Jones
March 2001

Introduction

Will the last person to leave church please turn off the lights?

The church is in trouble. No-one seriously disagrees with that. On current trends fewer than one in a hundred English people will be attending church by 2016. As Mike Riddell so aptly says, 'The Christian church is dying in the West.'[1] He backs up his assertion with the fact that '53,000 attenders are leaving the church in Europe and North America every week, and they are not coming back.'[2]

His is not a lone voice. The massive church-attendance survey published at the end of the 1990s showed that for the first time since the Dark Ages church attendance in England and Wales had fallen below 10% of the population. Commenting on the figures, Peter Brierley, who oversaw the survey, said: 'The trends in the current church-going numbers are frightening for those who care about the church and the gospel of Jesus Christ for which it stands. They suggest an indifference, a lack of understanding, commitment and interest perhaps unparalleled since Augustine came to these shores in 579 AD.'[3]

I am one of those who cares about the church. When I started the first edition of this book in the mid-1990s as the 'decade of evangelism' was getting into its stride, there was some optimism that with a little tinkering at the edges of how we do church, and greater commitment to outreach, we could turn the tide and see our churches growing again. This second edition is being written a year after the end of the decade, and I feel like a holidaymaker on Blackpool beach at low tide, where the sea is so far away I can barely make out the shoreline.

The dust has now settled and the headcount taken. Over the 'decade of evangelism' more than one million people left our churches. Despite the JIM (Jesus in Me) campaign (Remember that? It consisted of several million pounds'-worth of poster advertising in the early 1990s), *Minus to Plus* (the distribution of millions of evangelistic booklets to UK homes by evangelist Reinhart Bonkke), the Toronto Blessing, seeker services, Alpha courses, talk of revival, gold teeth, purpose-driven ministers and goodness knows what else, our churches are emptier now than they were in 1989. The time for tinkering at the edges of how we do church is surely well and truly over.

It's time to ask the question: why bother with the church at all? This is a question that is being increasingly asked by people in the church as well as outside it. It is certainly being asked by those who find the whole business of church a struggle. Is it worth the effort and energy? Maybe you're one of these people.

You're not alone. At the end of the 1990s another major survey was published, called *Gone but not Forgotten*.[4] This analysed why people stopped going to church. Readers were surprised that the least common reason given was loss of faith. Rather, people got bored, moved away, found other things taking up more time, or came to feel that church was irrelevant to the rest of their lives: in short, they ran out of reasons to bother with the church. And it seems churches ran out of reasons to bother with them. Startlingly, the report reveals that 92% of those who left the church in the 1990s were never asked why. Leslie Francis, one of the report's authors, comments: 'It is an indictment that so many leavers said that no-one seemed to notice they'd gone. That's careless.'[5]

The report says: 'If churches are to retain their members they need to take account of the difficulties people face in maintaining their faith … Are churches taking seriously the actual questions people are asking in late-modern society? Do churches encourage their members to express doubts and to ask hard-hitting questions? Do churches truly cater for those who are struggling with their faith?'[6] The answer – given the numbers leaving – seems to be 'Probably not'.

A church that listens to its strugglers not only helps them to maintain their faith and commitment, but equips itself better to reach out to those hanging on by their fingernails. 'The church that stands alongside people and supports them at times of need is most likely to help people maintain, or retrieve, their faith in the goodness of God,' says the report.[7]

Hidden in the church–attendance figures is another indication that people struggle to make the connection between their faith and church. Over the 1990s 1.6 million new people started attending church. But 2.8 million stopped. Maybe this indicates that we can capture people's interest, even intrigue them – perhaps through Alpha or a seeker service – but we can't engage their long-term commitment.

Whatever conclusion we draw from the statistics and the research, one thing is clear: the church is in trouble. I hope this book will be read by those struggling to maintain involvement in church. Perhaps you're looking for a reason to carry on. Read this book, wrestle with the issues and give it one more shot. Perhaps you're a churchgoer, leader, even minister, who would like to help to make church less of a struggle for people on the edge. Read on, think about what I say in relation to your own situation and make the appropriate connections.

I still believe that the church is central to God's plan to redeem the world, for reasons explained in chapters 2 and 3. But I do believe we need to ask some pretty fundamental questions about what the church should be like and what it's for. It is surely true that the church of the twenty-first century will be very different from the church of the twentieth.

So although the outline of the second edition of this book is the same as that of the first, every paragraph has been revisited. Some have been cut, some rewritten and some expanded. In the light of reviews and conversations, much has been added, including one whole new chapter and a conclusion that deals with the 'So what?' and 'What do I do now?' questions that I hope will arise for strugglers and church-lovers alike.

New to this edition is a chapter on how the church itself is struggling. Many of us find the church an awkward and painful place to be, partly because the church itself is struggling to find its place in a world that has changed out of all recognition over the past generation.

One of the most fundamental changes that few of us have taken on board is that the culture we live in no longer shares our view of the world. What Steve Turner says about art applies equally to society, morality, science, the whole of life: 'From the time of Constantine through to the Enlightenment, Christian ideas dominated art for the simple reason that the church had a powerful grasp over every aspect of life. There may well have been as many unregenerate people then as now, but they were unregenerate people who nevertheless understood their lives in terms of creation, fall and redemption. Painters routinely tackled subjects such as the Madonna and child, the crucifixion and the torments of hell.'[8]

Charting the history of Christianity in Britain since 1800, Callum Brown concludes that 'what emerges is a story not merely of church decline, but the end of Christianity as a means by which men and women, as individuals, construct their identities and their sense of "self"'.[9] He argues that through the Victorian era right up to the end of the 1950s, the Christian story provided the generally accepted explanation of life and especially of morality. It told us where we came from and how we should live – even if we never went near a church. It was the story that lay behind the stories told to us in the media, novels and movies. This is now no longer the case.

We'll pick up Brown's argument in chapter 7. But at the very least, it means that the church in Britain (and Western Europe, though maybe not yet the USA) finds itself in a missionary situation. If we go out into the street and speak to people in the language we use in church (however contemporary we feel that is) about the things we concern ourselves with in church, people will not have a clue what we're talking about or why it matters. We might as well be speaking Serbo-Croat for all the sense we'll make.

This is profoundly disturbing to Christians, and the cause of much bewilderment among ministers and church leaders. It is why many churches struggle to find a place in the bright new world of the new millennium, and why its struggles often make it an uncomfortable, even unpleasant place to be if we are searching for our own handle on reality in the flux that passes for the culture we live in. If the story of the world and our place in it that we learn at home, at school and college, through the media and from our friends is profoundly at odds with the story we're hearing in church, we'll find church a struggle.

Of course, there's a lot missing from this book. It is still not the final word on the church – no single book could be. And it is a book of questions rather than answers – though there are some suggestions and pointers to where some of the answers might lie. Something is wrong. Many of us feel it even if we can't put our finger on exactly what it is. I hope these pages will help us to tease out the right questions to be asking about the church in general, our own local churches in particular, and our individual roles in them.

This book is a journey, a voyage of discovery. Both church members and leaders, struggling to make a place of belonging for people in their neighbourhood, and those who are struggling to see why church matters at all, have things to learn from one another on this journey. So I hope that, whatever our view of the church, we will make room for other people's perspectives as we travel through this book. God's people are a wonderfully diverse bunch.

The most gratifying result of the first edition of this book as far as I'm concerned has been the number of people who've written to me or spoken to me about their church. Some ministers, some strugglers and all kinds of people in between have engaged me in debate about things in the book. Some have vehemently disagreed; others have thanked me for helping them make sense of the church. I hope this new edition – which takes account of many of those conversations – will continue the dialogue. Books aren't meant to be consumed like ice cream. They are one side of a conversation that each and every reader is invited to join. Authors – well, this one, certainly – toss words into the ether in the hope that someone will bounce them back with interest.

So write to me at IVP, email me at peckhamboy@ cwcom.net, visit the website www.ivpbooks.com, send a carrier pigeon or put a message in a bottle. Let's talk about the church and how we can help ours to reflect the New Testament's picture of a vibrant, life-affirming community of women and men drawn from every nation, tribe, social class and ethnic background, which helps people to encounter Jesus and to make sense of their lives in a turbulent and troubling world.

1 Stop the church, I want to get off

Week after week our church buildings are filled with the strains of singing. God's people, gathered together, sing of the joy of belonging to him and his church. True, most of our songs – especially the new ones – talk about *my* relationship with *my* God. But some also speak of our relationships with one another, about how the church is the place where God is at work, and how, through the church, God is going to change our land for good. Just turn to the index of any hymnbook for examples.

Those of us who are involved in leading what churches do Sunday by Sunday often look out on the sea of singing faces and assume that everyone is joining in, and that those who don't appear to be singing aren't doing so because they are distracted by their children or by someone coming in late at the back. It rarely enters our heads that some might not be singing because for them the words have an awfully hollow ring.

Why battle on?

Colin wasn't able to sing those songs any more. He came to London to see me, to take me to an exhibition and to seek refuge from his church. He was also due to visit a specialist counsellor to talk about his depression.

We'd known each other for the best part of ten years; we'd shared lots of walks and bottles of wine, good laughs and serious conversations about church and the life of faith. He was deeply in love with Jesus, and he was sharing his life with a group of Christians from a variety of backgrounds, playing a key role in the development of a church, and working alongside colleagues whose gifts complemented his own.

But Colin was also signed off work with depression, a condition caused by stress at work. He was a minister, and the stress was being caused by a senior colleague and the combined expectations of a hundred or so people. A major factor in his condition (and one that we'll return to later in this chapter) was that there was a contradiction between what his senior colleague said and how he was living. Colin found this increasingly difficult to reconcile with his faith in Jesus. Everyone at church was still singing the songs, but Colin found the taste of hypocrisy too bitter on his tongue.

'Time and time again over the past few weeks,' he said to me, 'I've asked myself, "Why do we carry on, when the church seems to do so much harm to people?" I'll never see things the same way again.'

Colin is not alone, of course, in his struggle with the church. For every ten or so smiling, satisfied singers in church on a Sunday morning, someone is struggling, either in the congregation or (more likely) at home, unable to face the congregation any more.

People like Madge. She was bright, a child of the manse who'd read drama at university. Struggling to fit in a church, she persevered until her marriage collapsed due to her husband's adultery. The church was embarrassed by her presence. She drifted away.

John worked for a lively parachurch organization for a year, then another, and then looked for work in the 'real world' (as he called it) as he tried to fathom out what to do in the long term. He joined a church but he didn't fit. He knew too much about church life to be an ordinary member, but not enough about that particular church to have a role. He had ideas and gifts, but he felt unwanted and frustrated. He came and went. Whenever he was asked about the direction the church was taking, he sounded cynical. People stopped asking him. He went, and didn't come back again.

An American Baptist leader, a pastor for over thirty years, learnt that because his daughter-in-law received contaminated blood products, his grandson was HIV positive. He turned to the family of God for support, but was met by fear, uncertainty and a coolness he'd never encountered before. His faith in Jesus is undiminished, but his faith in Jesus' people has taken something of a hammering. His family was being torn apart by Aids, but the family of God's people seemed incapable of responding with love and concern.

Douglas Kennedy, in his book *In God's Country: Travels in the Bible Belt, USA,* chronicles the ins and outs of American fundamentalism and televangelism. As well as describing the wackier end of this phenomenon, he also tells stories of people who have been left damaged by involvement with this scene.

One story illustrates the fact that sometimes it is not our choice, but that of our family, that can cause us problems with the church. A woman called Billie tells how her father, a feck-less drifter who moved from town to town working and preaching, put her and her sister in foster homes while he was travelling. Up to her eighteenth birthday, she lived in thirty-five different homes of families of a variety of Christian persuasions. Not surprisingly, she grew up confused. Her adult life was a catalogue of disasters: two failed marriages, poor health and the suicide of a boyfriend.

Reflecting on her life, she muses: 'I still wonder sometimes if God is punishing me for leaving the church ... Maybe all this was the Lord's way of getting back at me.' Kennedy comments: 'Suddenly, her addiction to menthol cigarettes, mail order catalogues and piles of nibbly food appeared to be the zenith of self-control when compared to the horror movie that has been her life.'[1]

We Christians, who believe that through Jesus God brings healing to people like Billie, would surely hope that she would find help among God's people. But though she still feels haunted by God and accountable to him, and guilty, though (it seems) through precious little fault of her own, the church is the last place she is likely to look for solace, support or friendship in her time of crisis, because of the way she was brought up and the model of faith and church involvement she has inherited from her father and her numerous foster families.

Jerry grew up in Africa and then the English Midlands, the son of missionary parents. His dad, a doctor, was dedicated and prayerful. But Jerry was lost. It seems no-one had considered his needs and expectations as he grew up seemingly shunted from continent to continent, unable to put roots down anywhere. He drifts around the edge of his church, unable to understand the world apart from the Christian story, but unable to commit himself wholeheartedly to a God who he believes played fast and loose with his childhood.

And so the stories go on: page after page of accounts of people who are attracted to Jesus, and who feel the need to have God in their lives. Some of them are trying to follow him, base their lives on his teaching and seek the strength of his Spirit, but they are not finding the church any help at all. Entering the community of people that is intended by God to be the place of healing and help is too often a harmful experience. Far from being a place of wholeness and peace, it is a cause of pain and trouble. The world is awash with casualties, people damaged by church.

Of course, there are those for whom church is, all things considered (and after all, nothing's perfect), a really good experience. Within the people of God they find friends, affirming relationships, fulfilling spheres of service, and a deepening understanding of God and love for him. Perhaps this is still the overwhelming majority of churchgoers. Their stories will be told in succeeding chapters of this book.

Why is this happening?

But why are there increasing numbers of people for whom church is, on balance, more negative than positive – a growing band of 'used-to-be' members of churches? A fellow minister recently said he was convinced that there was a vast 'congregation' of Bible-reading, Jesus-loving people who just didn't happen to go to church on a Sunday or take any active part in the life of their local church, of whatever hue. These people, when asked by MORI or by church visitors doing door-to-door work, say, 'I'm a Christian, but I don't go to church. I read my Bible; I try to do what God wants at work and home – but I don't see the point of church.'

No doubt, if pressed, these people would describe an experience similar to those detailed in the last few pages. Perhaps they have never seen the point of joining a church. 'And after all,' they say, 'I've got my Bible and a load of Christian books and tapes; I can pray; I can watch services on TV; I can call up Christians on the phone or internet. Why go to church?' Perhaps with a note of understandable bitterness, they'd say, 'I want nothing to do with the church. They're all hypocrites who do more harm than good.'

Many of these in our increasingly mobile society are people who have moved several times because of studies and jobs. Perhaps in their home town they were well integrated into a church, able to take the rough with the smooth. But as they have moved around, their enthusiasm and energy to make a fresh start in church have waned. They have found it harder in each new church to begin again, forging relationships and finding a place and a role for themselves among a group of people who seem to have known each other for a long time and can sometimes send out unintentional unwelcoming signals to newcomers. After all, when everything is working nicely and everyone has a role, it can be disruptive to bring a new person, with a new way of doing things, into the group.

Aaron was interviewed for the book *Gone but not Forgotten*. He'd moved home and failed to find a church. 'I've just sort of faded out and stopped going. I don't know if it's because I've moved to a new house, and just haven't found a church, or if it's just because I've become less interested.'[2] Even if you can summon the enthusiasm to look for a new church once you've moved, you've then got the hurdle of crossing the threshold. 'I didn't go to church', says Tom, 'because I didn't dare go to this church and see all the new people.'[3]

When I first came to London to work as a journalist, I too drifted away from church. I'd been prayer secretary in my Christian Union, done detached Christian youth work on a housing estate in Salford, and sung in numerous churches around the North West of England. But when I arrived in London with a new job and a new place to live, I had the chance to make a new start. Would church be part of that new life? For many months it wasn't – partly because I couldn't really be bothered to look for a church and partly because I wondered if I believed any of this stuff any more. Then at a party I bumped into an old friend who asked me which church I was going to, and invited me to his. He made sure that when I turned up, plenty of people made me very welcome, included me in their activities and gave me a sense of belonging to a group of people who cared about me although they knew very little about me. I stayed.

It is easy for those of us who love church, and have found membership of it to be a wholly or mainly beneficial experience, to dismiss these stories as the whinging of malcontents or the unfortunate and untypical experiences of a tiny minority. After all, we say (with some justification), you can't blame the church for dysfunctional families or for the choices that some people make against the advice of their friends or the teaching of Scripture.

But that is not the most helpful response. A little something in these stories ought to make us ask ourselves and our churches: 'Why is this happening?' If we're honest, we've all had moments in our own involvement with church when we've exclaimed in tones of mounting exasperation, 'Why do I bother?' After a Sunday morning service where I have proclaimed the love and mercy of God, I've stood in my kitchen stunned and shell-shocked from the comments, the carping attitudes and the actions of some Christians in my congregation. And I've said to Linda, as she's brought the consoling sherry, 'There must be more to church than this!'

At this stage, I want to suggest four weaknesses the church often exhibits that can lead to people being damaged by involvement with it.

For the in-crowd only

The first is that the church is an unwelcoming place to outsiders. Oh, it's not that people don't say hello to visitors; it's that visitors are expected to get the hang of what's going on instantly, and that doesn't happen.

Consider this lengthy story about one woman's experience on her first visit to church for some time. As you read it, think about the strangers coming into your church and ask if it is possible that they feel as she does. Perhaps you'll recognize your own experience in her story.

Polly wandered nervously through the door from the lobby. She'd been greeted politely but awkwardly by the middle-aged man at the entrance. He had handed her a folded A4 sheet, said 'Welcome', and directed her with a combination of sweeping hand gestures and curt, barely audible phrases to the door behind him.

Through the door it was chilly. A few people milled around the table at the back of the room. Ones and twos around the hall were sitting silently, looking down at their laps. Gaggles of twos and threes and fours were chatting in corners and at the ends of the rows of seats. At the front, someone was putting a vase of flowers on the table in the centre. Two or three musicians were gathered around a music stand, giggling.

More people came in through the door. They spread out like a multicoloured stain from the corner of the room, filling seats (mainly at the back), greeting friends, and putting books and papers under chairs. A few smiled at Polly; wan smiles of politeness rather than warm grins of welcome, but nice all the same.

Suddenly (or so it seemed to Polly, who had discovered a great interest in the way walls joined ceilings in the corners of rooms), the musicians started playing, and everyone stood up and broke into song. Polly looked round at the people near her. Everyone was staring at the front wall of the hall. Gazing forward, her eyes were met by the words of the song projected on to a big screen behind the band.

The tune was pleasant enough, but the words were unfamiliar. As one song ended, it was replaced by another, the hands of an unseen person moving the acetates on and off the overhead projector with consummate skill. Polly didn't know any of the songs; it had been a while since she'd been in church. But she made a half-hearted attempt to join in so as not to stand out too much from those around her.

She looked round at the faces of those near her. Some were in rapt attention to the words; some were frowning, lips curled into what looked like a sneer; others were paying closer attention to the floor or to their neighbour, their children or their spouse than to the words on the screen.

Everyone sat down. At the front, a man in a check jacket said 'Good morning', offered a word of welcome, especially to anyone new this morning, and announced the next song. For the next hour Polly stood to listen while others sang, sat to hear people praying or talking about things happening later that day or through the week, stood to put her money in the offering-bag and sat to listen to the preacher. What he said was interesting. 'I wish I could talk to him more about that,' she thought.

The service ended. Polly sat. People started moving. All around her, men and women greeted each other, talked about various things, laughed, looked serious, shook hands, hugged and moved on. For five minutes Polly sat. People squeezed past her, smiling and nodding. She stood up, sidled to the end of the row, and started walking to the back of the room, glancing back at the people. In the lobby the preacher was deep in conversation with a middle-aged man. He held out his hand, half looking in Polly's direction. She hung back, hesitated, and finally shook his hand and walked back into the street.

Superficial words of greeting from the front and the odd smile as you pass a visitor by do not constitute a welcome. Many people come into church because they want to find out about Jesus, to get to know him better, or to find somewhere in this world where they can feel a sense of belonging. All too often they are greeted by well-meaning, polite indifference.

Others come out of a sense of need – a recent bereavement, the break-up of a relationship, a house move, changes at work, perhaps a niggling feeling that there must be more to life than getting up, going to work, coming home and watching TV. For some, church is an obvious place to look for 'something more'. To be greeted with indifference tells them that they were wrong. Church has no answers to anything; it's just a club for insiders.

It's possible that Polly would have returned a few times to that church in the hope that she could get the conversation she wanted with the minister. The statistics from the 1990s suggest that we can attract people. But they also strongly indicate that we can't keep them. Ultimately Polly will drift away because no-one makes her feel welcome, no-one gives her an indication that she might well belong with this group of people.

Sometimes other organizations have a great deal to teach the church about being welcoming. A sports club often welcomes new members far better than a church does. Someone takes the trouble to explain how things work and when the facilities are open, and even introduces you to people who might play a game with you.

Mary came to our church in the early 1960s. At the time, she was the only black person in a congregation of over a hundred. Week in, week out, she came and went and no-one spoke to her. The secretary welcomed everyone from the front, but no-one welcomed her in person. She says that she stayed because no-one told her not to come back!

Eventually the pastor spoke to her at the door. They got to know each other. One day he asked her, 'How come, when West Indian people come for dedications [something Baptists do to families with new babies], they don't stay?'

Mary replied with disarming understatement: 'The people here seem a bit selfish. They don't greet strangers.'

The miracle is that Mary stayed, and through the years of the church's decline she remained loyal. Now she is a leader of the church and is seeing it grow again. One thing her experience of thirty years ago taught her is that new people need to be greeted, welcomed and genuinely accepted if they are going to stay and make their home here.

It is, of course, a simple and obvious point. We expect Christians at least to be polite and civil, to be aware that strangers feel awkward in a new environment, and to do their best to put them at their ease. But it is amazing how many churches appear unfriendly and unwelcoming to newcomers. In this we reflect not the love and concern of Jesus, but the indifference of a culture that has forgotten its manners, and lost the ability to be polite and courteous to all and sundry. It is something we shall return to time and again in this book.

But it also indicates something about the types of relationships we foster in the church. Is my congregation merely a

group of my friends, people like me whom I really get on
with? If it is, it is unlikely to be a very welcoming place to
people who aren't like me. As we shall see in chapters 2 and 3,
the church should be a place where relationships form across
the barriers that divide people – class, race, gender, taste.

You'd better believe it

The second reason church can be an off-putting place to so
many people is that Christians, and especially Christian
leaders, can appear arrogant. We know the truth about God
and the meaning of life, we know what's wrong with the
world and what needs to happen to put it right, and we have
the revelation of the mind of God on our communion tables
and in our hands and handbags (the Bible). And we're not
afraid to tell people that. And this too can make us feel very
unwelcoming. What Polly hears as she tries to join in the
singing and praying and listening to the sermon is that she is
not as good as the people sitting around her, that she doesn't
know the secret everyone else does.

Of course, it's right to be unashamed of the gospel. Jesus
told us to get out into the world and talk about him. The
trouble is that we often come across to people as having it all
sewn up. Life is a breeze. Jesus is the answer; now, what's your
question? Well, actually, don't ask questions; just believe what
we say.

When people, especially Christians, do ask questions, we
raise our eyebrows in alarm. The reason for this is that often
we don't know the answers, and we feel that if we can't give
answers we shall lose our ability to control what happens to us
and to others. This is especially true of ministers and Christian
leaders, but it's also true of Christians generally. Questions are
a threat to faith and order. This is one of the reasons the
Pharisees and other leaders of Jesus' day found the carpenter
from Galilee such a pain; he was always questioning why they
did things the way they did.

When people, especially Christians, say, 'How can God allow all those people to die on that ferry that sank?', or 'I'm having a difficult time reconciling what look like contradictions in Scripture', or 'Sometimes I'm not sure whether God really hears my prayers', we get nervous. We close ranks and say, 'We've not got any problems with these things: here are the explanations. This is what we teach here. This is what we all believe. The problem is with you: you must just believe what we tell you, as everyone else does.'

Of course, it is never said in so many words or expressed so crudely. It is, rather, intimated in tuts and furrowed brows and looks of deep concern. It's expressed in being taken to one side – because 'we're so concerned about you' – and in being invited to join an 'enquirers' group', or to have some counselling or an opportunity to talk about your problems with a leader or pastor.

What's required is not remedial action but honesty. We don't need to offer therapy or deliverance or even a course in Christian basics. Many of us have already been on a course of Christian basics. We know what the faith is about, but we still struggle with some issues. Churches need to offer openness and a willingness to walk with people through their questions. We need to reassure people that life is a journey of discovery, that asking questions and expressing doubts are part of faith, and that simple solutions to deep problems are not on offer.

The rock band U2 have had an ambiguous, ambivalent relationship with the church. Part of the reason for this is undoubtedly that they have asked questions, expressed thoughts and articulated doubts that have not been well received by Christians. They are open to ideas from all sorts of quarters, some of which Christians think are highly suspect. It is also true that the lifestyle of a rock group doesn't sit comfortably with membership of the average church.

U2 were hailed in the early 1980s as a Christian band. Their song 40 is the Psalm of that number set to a driving rock tune. In the 1990s, with the albums *Achtung Baby*, *Zooropa*, *Pop* and most recently *All that You Can't Leave Behind*, Christians debated whether the band had 'gone off the rails' or whether they were still writing and performing out of a Christian worldview. Certainly the evidence of *All that You Can't Leave Behind* would suggest very strongly that Bono's lyrics are written out of a profoundly biblical view of things by a man deeply immersed in his world.[4]

But they certainly weren't going to church – except when they were in San Francisco (of which more in a later chapter) – so the conclusion that they were no longer walking with the Lord seemed obvious to many. But in his biography of the band, covering the period of the Zoo TV tour, US journalist Bill Flanagan keeps coming back to the subject of the band's faith, describing their albums and tour as a kind of spiritual odyssey. At one point Bono describes his antics on the tour – especially the character of Machphisto – as being like C. S. Lewis's *Screwtape Letters* or even Ecclesiastes in action or set to music.[5]

We shall return to this later in the book. But at this point I want to note something that Bono's dad, Bob Hewson, recalls of the time when his boy and other members of the band joined a charismatic church in their native Dublin. 'He became mixed up with – I don't know what they called themselves, but they were some kind of Bible group. I've always been a little cagey of those people who say they have all the answers.'[6] He sees Bono's subsequent pilgrimage as a maturing of whatever faith he has, not as its overthrow.

One of the great weaknesses of the church is that it is often perceived as a place where thinking is discouraged and people are spoonfed a series of beliefs by leaders who've got only answers and no questions. Another rock singer, Joan Osborne, tackled this head-on when, in an interview in *Mojo* magazine, she said, 'The idea of embracing the fall from grace is important to me because fundamentalists, not only in America, but in cultures across the world, have an agenda which reduces human beings ... If you're going to be pure and good you can't be sexy, you can't be creative, you can't think for yourself, you have to be an obedient little sheep.' A number of the songs on her album *Relish* explore this former Catholic's fall from grace and her struggles with a God who still seems to be hanging around.

In a day that puts a premium on individual freedom and choice, on thinking things through and making decisions for oneself, it is a severe weakness if the church is known as a place where thinking is off limits. The Bible suggests that God wants us to come and enter into a dialogue with him about how we should live. In that case, the church should be a place where that dialogue is possible. And far from 'reducing human beings', God wants people to grow into the image of his Son, to become complete, whole and fully rounded, as he is.

The Bible is full of examples of God asking people to work it out for themselves within the framework he provides. Note that it's a framework, not a straitjacket. 'Come now, let us argue it out,' he urges the people of Israel through the prophet Isaiah (1:18). The classic Old Testament example, of course, is Ecclesiastes, a whole book devoted to grappling with the issues of life and meaning, God and his relationship to us and our world. But there are also countless psalms where the poet wrestles with his experience and the doctrines of his worshipping community, and notes a reality gap – the most cogent of these being Psalm 73. (Why not read it now and join the debate?)

But it is Jesus' teaching style that really emphasizes the fact that God wants to enter into discussion with us and to lead us into an understanding of his truth as we dialogue with him, think through what we're told, and apply it to our lives and experience – with his help. The parables of Jesus are fine examples of such a teaching method. Jesus tells a story or throws out a thought that is open-ended, inviting his hearers to mull over what he says, to think about it, to question it and to see if it has the ring of truth about it. If it does, he invites us back for more. We see this clearly in Mark 4, where Jesus delivers the parable of the sower. 'Let anyone with ears to hear listen!' he says at the end (Mark 4:9). The crowd splits. Some leave, thinking, 'Well, that didn't amount to much, did it?' Others hang around and enter into a dialogue with Jesus. 'What was the parable about?' they ask him (see Mark 4:10).

Having explained the parable (but still leaving his hearers to work out which kind of soil they are), he goes on to talk about the fact that there is nothing secret about what he's doing; for those who are prepared to look, listen and think about what they see and hear, it's plain. He is a very non-directive teacher, inviting his disciples to explore what the life of faith might be like.

The church ought to be the place where the likes of Bono (and he is like countless others on the fringe of the church, only more famous and richer!) can work through their questions, doubts, angst and uncertainties without being labelled heretics, backsliders or troublemakers. In a later chapter we shall look at how a sense of belonging to the church precedes believing everything the church stands for. Faith grows out of feeling accepted, rather than feeling that we have to sign a declaration of belief before we're allowed through the door.

Do as we say, don't do as we do

The third reason people struggle with the church is that Christians, and especially Christian leaders, fail to live up to what they preach. This brings us back to Colin, whom we met at the beginning of this chapter. His senior colleague taught and preached Christian values, especially good relationships at home and honesty among the people of God. But his own marriage was failing, and he wasn't open about this situation to the other leaders. Neither was he open about a relationship with another woman that was heading for an affair. In fact, the few who knew anything about it, including Colin, were bullied into silence by their spiritual leader, who said it would damage the weaker members of the congregation who looked up to him if even a hint of what was going on slipped out. How often churches are run like shabby little empires built on manipulation and fear! It is little wonder Colin struggled.

In the States the scandals surrounding TV evangelists like Jimmy Swaggart and Jim Bakker have tended to make many people cynical about the claims of Christians to be on to something real and valuable. 'If that's how the spokesmen for the movement carry on, you can keep it,' is a common reaction.

Church leaders will never be perfect, and church members should not expect it. There are dangers when leaders and preachers take or are given too much authority. Some even claim the authority of prophets and apostles and warn that speaking against them is 'striking the Lord's anointed'. The danger is twofold. First, they cease to be accountable and gain too much power, especially over the lives of the vulnerable and easily led. Secondly, others, often those on the edge of the church, assume that such posturing is ludicrous and that the faith of such people can't be up to all that much.

Leaders – mainly full-time people such as ministers and evangelists, but also 'lay' leaders such as elders, deacons, lay readers, youth leaders, and so on – need to be more transparent, honest about their struggles, humble about their abilities and needs, and healthy in their level of self-deprecation and self-criticism. We need to model a questing, questioning faith, a life of pilgrimage that faces doubts and darkness.

We need, too, to be upfront about our uncertainties as well as our certainties. As I grow in my Christian faith, I am certain of less. But that 'less' is the core of the faith, and about that I am more and more certain. This core is about God revealed in Scripture as Father, Son and Holy Spirit; about salvation as a gift received by faith in Jesus; about the Bible as the trustworthy and authoritative story of God's work in the world;

about new life through the cross of Jesus, brought to us by the indwelling Holy Spirit. Everything else is a matter of opinion and debate, things to be pondered, held lightly, and weighed and tested by experience. The core of the faith is worth dying for. The periphery is not worth losing friends over.

If a leader models a faith of total certainties, with no doubts, no grey areas and no question marks, and has a crisis of faith, a period of calamity that causes him publicly to question what he believes, a lot of people will go down with him. And a lot of people on the margin of the church or struggling to believe will have their suspicions or scepticism about the faith confirmed.

Some time ago, I stumbled into a valley of the shadow of death that was deep and unsettling. A close friend, a member of the church I was pastoring, who was six months pregnant and beginning to feel the excitement of being a first-time mother, caught a cold and died. Her son was left fighting for his life, fourteen weeks premature, in an incubator. Her husband was left teetering between grief at her death and joy at the birth of his son. Her friends in church were shattered, confused, angry, and sad beyond their ability to cope.

I walked on the beach at Hope Cove in Devon, one of my favourite parts of the world, and a place Ellie would have loved. I dared God to show up. I shouted at him. I demanded explanations and I wept freely. I was angry and strident like Job, and blubbed like a child.

Ellie died on a Thursday, and I had to preach to a grieving people on the following Sunday. I wanted to know what to say. God was silent. I was lost for words. But as I walked on the beach and cried and shouted, I began to feel the presence of a companion, a strong presence but a gentle one, like the arms of a father wrapping a small child in a big fluffy towel. I found the words in that experience and in Isaiah 40 – a great portrait of God given to a people who felt abandoned.

Those words gave shape to my grief, and voice to my

confusion. When I stood on Sunday to speak through the tears, I did not mount a defence of the providence of God, nor did I articulate a theology of suffering. I expressed my profound difficulties in grasping what was happening, and in seeing any light in this dark pit. I said that my major feeling was pain and sadness, and that that was my offering to God today, my worship on this Lord's Day.

I went on to say that I felt acutely that life was like one of those magic-eye pictures: no matter how hard I stared at it, all I could make out were jumbled, jarring shapes that added up to nothing. The Bible – especially Isaiah 40 with its majestic portrait of the creator and sustainer of the universe – told me that God was working to a plan. I believed that was true, though that morning I couldn't see it.

I said that I had found God in my walk along the beach, not as someone with a clutch of answers, but as a comforting presence who wept and shared my grief. I had found him in the Scriptures as I read, and I had found him in other people as we wept together. I had felt his hand supporting me when I thought I could not go on. I spoke falteringly, and tried to articulate not only my grief but also the grief of my congregation.

After preaching that sermon, I was greeted by a young woman, a single mum, recently divorced and thus acquainted with pain and struggle, who said it was the best sermon she'd heard me preach. She also said that, although she hadn't really known Ellie, she'd be coming to the funeral because Ellie so clearly meant a lot to our church and she wanted to be a part of that kind of family. Shortly afterwards, she became a member, and is now actively involved in the life of the church.

It is vital that, as churches, we make room for the dark side, the down side, the desperate struggles of people in the teeth of life's dangers and difficulties. Sin means that our world is a messy, uncomfortable place. Faith helps us to live in that world; it does not lift us out of it.

Even when life is good and calm, leaders really ought to

come across as people who think about life and faith and how the two impact on each other. Douglas Kennedy tells of meeting 'Brother Birt', a black minister in Alabama. He was clearly quite impressed by this modest, unassuming man. 'He came across as a serious guy who was serious about his faith, his work and the people he ministered to; a man who may never have been outside of the South, but who had still encountered a great deal of life's manifold complexities and had thought long and hard about the contemporary implications of Christianity in his own small patch of the world.'[7] Would that all church leaders were more like Brother Birt!

Split personality

A fourth weakness that we are prone to is compartmentalization. We split life up into fragments: sacred and secular, spiritual and earthly, evangelism and social action, work and worship. As individuals we hear about things on Sunday but we fail to see them through into our lives on Monday. As leaders, teachers and preachers, we so often fail to make the connection between what happens in our church on Sunday and what our congregations do in the world during the week. We give the impression that Christians can somehow live in a bubble, insulated and isolated from the world around them, immune to its trials and tribulations.

In his provocative little book *So Long, Farewell and Thanks for the Church* Morris Stuart suggests that many people – whom he describes as 'refugees' – have left the church because it fails to live up to the ideals of its founder in precisely this area of seeing our preaching and praying through into our lives, not just in church, but also in the world.

'As long as seasons of "renewal" and "refreshment" in the church are not matched by fundamental and far-reaching changes in society,' he writes, 'the flow of refugees will continue, and the constant claims of divine refreshing will increasingly have a hollow ring.'[8] Stuart goes on to point out

that 'The Hutu and Tutsi in Rwanda and Burundi are
engaging in one of the most tragic episodes of genocide this
century. This in a region which only a generation before had
been blessed by the East African revival.'[9]

Ouch! These words sting. He probably overstates the case.
After all, God does move in renewal of people and refreshment of his church, which then meets greater opposition in a
society that refuses to change. One example that comes to
mind is the Ethiopia of the Menghistu era, where many new
converts lost their lives simply for becoming Christians. And
one has only to think of the monumental changes in Eastern
Europe, and to talk to Christians from that part of the world
about the role that prayer played in all these changes, to realize
that the picture is far from simple.

Nevertheless, it is almost certainly true that people are put
off the faith we profess because we are otherworldly, and unin-
terested in the worlds of work, politics and community that
people live in. We talk a lot about salvation, inner healing,
peace and prosperity as spiritual experiences, but little about
how following Jesus changes our attitude to our work, our
community, the way we vote and the way we use the world's
resources.

It is a cliché to say that people today, especially those under
forty, are more attracted to causes than to institutions.
Politicians have recruited stand-up comedians and rock singers
in what smacks of a last-ditch effort to persuade the young to
register and use their vote, and to stem the drift of people
away from our democratic processes. People don't join unions,
political parties or tenants' associations any more. We get
involved in causes: we join the anti-road lobby to stop a
bypass, or demonstrate against live animal exports, animal
testing or GM crops. We bring Seattle, Gothenburg and Genoa
to a standstill in protest at the effects of globalization on the
world's poor – even if we're not sure what the alternative
might be. We are more likely to become school governors to

influence our own child's education than to stand for election as a local councillor to contribute to the education of every child in the neighbourhood.

All this means that the church has got to be a place where the world and people's concerns about it are taken seriously and addressed. It is no good preaching week in, week out, about speaking in tongues, sanctification, or how to praise the Lord with the latest Spring Harvest tape, if we aren't also preaching about how to be Christians at work, what God thinks and feels about the world we live in, and what kind of politics honours the King of kings.

It is frequently in small groups that meet during the week that Christians are able to thrash these issues out, and to wrestle with what Scripture is telling them about their lives, God and the real world. Church home groups, made up of people from all walks of life, of all ages and varying experiences, are vital crucibles for forging real, life-affirming, community-changing faith of the kind so many people in our world are looking for.

A number of Christians who struggled with church in the past joined the church I'm involved with because we have projects that offer non-vocational training to people without jobs, help adults learn to read and write, and provide daycare for people living with mental-health problems. It's not the final word, but it is the beginning of the conversation.

They are also there because in small groups they are able to bring their concerns about work. Jack, for instance, working for a housebuilder, was concerned to maintain his integrity in the face of cost-cutting measures that involved substituting cheaper materials in some of the schemes he was working on. Was this compromising safety? Should he be opposing this trend? If so, how? His home group helped him to think about the issue and supported him as he made his stand. His difficult time at work was easier to cope with because of the backing of his home group.

There is no reason why other home groups can't function like this. All it needs is for ministers and church leaders to relax their agenda and allow the concerns of members to influence what the groups do.

Douglas Kennedy speaks of the pivotal role the church played in the civil-rights movement in the American South in the 1960s. He tells of lunching at a church in Enterprise, Alabama, and afterwards of singing old-style spirituals. One particular song 'reminded those in need that the hellishness of daily life can be countered through "just a little talk with Jesus"'. Kennedy goes on to reflect that the spirituality that these churches have evolved is not, however, otherworldly. Rather, the intensely personal and emotional nature of the worship, founded on a direct relationship with Jesus, countered the message about being second-class citizens that most black people received every day from the world around them.

'No wonder, therefore,' says Kennedy, 'that the civil rights movement of the 1960s was led, in part, by black ministers who frequently cited Christian principles as a subtext to their civil disobedience. To them, Jesus was not simply a saviour to turn to in moments of crisis. He was also a great moral hero; the ultimate spiritual leader when it came to matters of equality and humanitarian principles.'[10]

So it is possible for Christians to live integrated rather than compartmentalized lives, bringing together the sacred and secular, the realms of the spirit and the flesh, church and world. It is possible for churches to speak on Sunday of things that affect the lives of their members on Monday, and to help those people to apply Scripture to their daily lives at work and home. It isn't easy. But we were never told it would be.

A community of sinners

These four weaknesses are real. They infect most churches, if not all, to some degree. Many churches are aware of them and seek to counter them through a variety of means. Just being aware of them is often sufficient to ensure that some or all of the members do something to overcome their effects.

But these weaknesses should not stop people joining the church. After all, we are drawn to Jesus because in him we find someone who accepts the fact that we make mistakes, and who welcomes us even though we are unattractive, selfish, bigoted, fragmented people. We are damaged by life, and we are attracted to Jesus because he offers to make us whole again. We are falling apart, and Jesus offers to put us together again. We are weighed down by the expectations of others as well as by our own expectations, and Jesus says, 'Come to me, all you that are weary and are carrying heavy burdens, and I will give you rest' (Mathew 11:28).

Not surprisingly, when we come into church we find a group of people like us, people who are broken, lonely, awkward, selfish and damaged. We find people who are at various stages of being put back together again by Jesus and for whom involvement in the church is a vital part of that repair process – a process in which we become more welcoming, better able to live with uncertainty, and less compartmentalized, more integrated people.

But it takes time. I think it was Eugene Peterson who said, 'Churches are groups of sinners led by sinners.' We must never forget that fact in our consideration of what the church is and what it should be, and in our expectations about how the church will function and what it will do for us.

Church will always have its down side. There will inevitably be clashes, harsh words, bad attitudes and unkind actions. This is not a counsel of despair. It is a recognition that where there are sinners, there is sin, and that sin manifests itself in the way we treat one another and in the random events that afflict us and throw us off course. But where there is Jesus, there is also grace in abundance to counter sin and its effects.

These two facts above all else – including a bad experience of church – should mould our expectations and fuel our determination to make belonging to the people of God work for our good and for the good of the communities we live in. For, as we shall see in the next chapter, it is what Jesus intended for those who love him and who want to follow him in our all too messy world.

2 Yes, but what is it for?

Ask the proverbial person on the Clapham omnibus (which does still run from central London to the trendy South London spot) what the church is, and they will almost inevitably start telling you about buildings – perhaps the one they saw a televised royal wedding in. No-one who has been involved with a church on a regular basis will give you anything like so definite an answer – except to say, of course, that the church isn't the building, it's the people.

Ask the proverbial person on the Clapham omnibus what the church is *for*, and they won't have the faintest idea, beyond perhaps suggesting that it's an elaborate job-creation scheme for blokes who like wearing frocks, and that it's pretty good for tourism!

But knowing what the church is for is vital if we're going to ally ourselves with it. After all, to use a slightly trivial example, we don't buy a major consumer durable – fridge, washing-machine, computer, car – without knowing what it does, how to get the best out of it and what it's going to cost to buy and run it. It is amazing how few of us do anything approaching a similar analysis with our churches – though, given the state of many of them, it's just as well we don't.

But do it now. Stop reading and ask yourself, 'If my

church disappeared tomorrow, would I miss it? Would my church miss me if I disappeared?' Be specific. What would I miss? How would not being at church affect my life at home and at work? By doing this, you are beginning to think about what the church is for.

It's for worship, isn't it?

When we look at what the church was for in the New Testament, what we discover could well surprise (even shock) you and most of the people who attend your church on Sundays. Of course, it might also delight and thrill you, and fill you with a sense of wonder and longing to be involved in such an outfit (I hope so!). And if you don't go to church, what we discover together could well transform your perception of what church actually is and maybe send you off in search of one that is struggling to fit the picture you've been shown.

Some time ago the New Testament scholar Howard Marshall raised a few eyebrows and ruffled a few feathers – certainly in the Bible-college seminar group I was a part of at the time – with an article suggesting that the early Christians did not meet together to worship.[1]

One of the dominant images of the church in the mind of the faithful and the undecided alike is that church is about worship, and that worship is mainly to do with singing. BBC TV call their weekly Sunday-evening foray into church (which is the closest millions come to actually attending one) *Songs of Praise*. Whenever the media cover church affairs, they invariably centre on a row over a new hymnbook or liturgy.

Ask excited, committed church members what they like about their church, and more often than not their description begins with the worship. They wax lyrical about the wonderful songs that are sung, the quality of the music and the liveliness of the participation. Churches that are described as 'successful' (whatever that word means when applied to church life!) are nearly always places with a worship group and a worship leader – often full-time – with a style of worship that blends a steady diet of modern worship songs with a few carefully chosen old hymns.

Increasing numbers of churches or groups are springing up where the emphasis is on music, performance and multimedia presentations of various kinds. Here, the congregation participates less by joining in than by listening, thinking, meditating on and responding to the themes being communicated from the stage. This in many ways is a return to the set-piece cathedral services where choirs and organists blended with liturgists and preachers to produce a worship experience for the congregation to watch and enjoy and, all being well, to learn from and be built up by. Such gatherings often enable people to encounter the mystery of God in ways that don't happen in your conventional sing-along, all-join-in church meeting. We'll pick up this idea later in the chapter.

Judging a church by its music is, of course, not a new phenomenon, and not one that is associated only with new or charismatic churches. For centuries, not only cathedrals, but all kinds of churches, from staid Baptist to off-the-wall Pentecostal, have boasted of their singing group, choir, choral tradition or whatever. Many pop singers began life in church groups.

Of course, this focus on singing is not universally popular among church members. My friend Anthony hates it. He doesn't like the music, and he can't join in – 'Not that I'd want to, you understand!' – because he can't read. My friend Geraldine doesn't like it either. She's tone deaf, was constantly made fun of at school because she couldn't hit a single right note, and has hated joining in music ever since. Both like to listen, though, to others singing.

Lots of other people find the current popular diet of music in church to be bland and soulless. 'It's wall-to-wall Radio 2 muzak,' says Chris. Those who argue that modern worship songs will bring the young into church clearly haven't listened to what the young listen to. Graham Kendrick might be a great hymnwriter, but he isn't contemporary in the way U2, REM, Limp Biscuit, Coldplay, Dido and even the Spice Girls are.

A recent Radio 1 poll of the all-time top 100 pop songs put Oasis' 'Wonderwall' at number one, Nirvana's 'Smells like Teen Spirit' at two and Prodigy's 'Firestarter' third – none of it music of a style you'll hear in the average church! Recent polls of the best albums ever or the most influential pop and rock performers in *Mojo*, *Q* and *NME* confirm the yawning chasm between what's on people's stereos and what we sing in churches.

It is also the case that younger people these days don't go overboard on participatory activities. Most of the hymnwriters and leaders of today's church grew up in the 1950s, 1960s and 1970s and came to faith in the midst of an explosion of 'body life' in the churches. Everyone wanted to join in, participate, have a role in getting things done. They have been succeeded by a generation which, for good or ill, takes a more detached view of participation, hangs back from involvement, wants a few, genuine relationships, and does not want to be asked to sing with strangers. There are some notable exceptions to this, of course. Soul Survivor events, for instance, attract large numbers of teenagers who appear happy to join in corporate singing – though many of the same young people don't sing the same songs in their home churches!

But whichever side we take in the 'modern versus traditional hymns' debate, we're not talking about worship in the New Testament sense or about what the early church did when it met, according to Howard Marshall. Some people, led by so-called new or house churches that sprang up in the UK in the 1970s and 1980s, have the idea that we must recapture the practices and quality of life of the early church. For them, worship is a key part of the menu. But these 'restorationists' have, according to Marshall, misread the text.

Marshall looked at the way New Testament writers used the language traditionally associated with religious gatherings in both Judaism and paganism; words like 'worship', 'service', 'praise', 'sacrifice'.

For example, the Greek verb *leitourgeō* (meaning 'serve' or 'worship') and related words, used in the surrounding culture of performing duties towards God, occur fifteen times in the New Testament (which was originally written in Greek). Six of these refer to what the Jewish priests did in the temple. Four of them refer to Christians giving aid to needy people (Romans 15:27; 2 Corinthians 9:12; Philippians 2:25, 30), one to evangelism (Romans 15:16), one to secular rulers' service to society (Romans 13:6), and two to the help given by angels to God's people (Hebrews 1:7, 14). Only once is the word used by a New Testament writer to speak of what Christians did when they gathered together (Acts 13:2) and even then it seems that only five church members were involved, not the whole church.

Marshall finds the same to be true of most of the key Greek words, leading him to conclude that 'although the whole activity of Christians can be described as the service of God and they are engaged throughout their lives in worshipping him, yet this vocabulary is not applied in any specific way to Christian meetings'.[2]

The Australian historian, Robert Banks, agrees. In his major study of Paul's idea of community, he says, 'One of the most puzzling features of Paul's understanding of *ekklēsia* [the Greek word for 'church'] for his contemporaries, whether Jews or Gentiles, must have been his failure to say that a person went to church primarily to worship. Not once in all his writings does he suggest that this is the case. Indeed it could not be, for he held a view of "worship" that prevented him from doing so.'[3]

Worship in the early church was a 24/7 activity, a way of life, something the believer did twenty-four hours a day, seven days a week, not a special activity undertaken once a week in a holy place on a holy day. The key text here is Romans 12:1: 'I appeal to you therefore, brothers and sisters, by the mercies of God, to present your bodies as a living sacrifice, holy and acceptable to God, which is your spiritual worship.' This sentence bristles with the language of worship, language that as a Jew Paul would have applied primarily to what happened in the temple. But as a Christian, Paul uses these words to describe our everyday lifestyle, and not holy-day rituals.

This sea change in the understanding of worship was rooted in the life and teaching of Jesus. He lambasted the religious folk of his day for paying attention to the fine detail of religious observance, such as tithing the herbs used to season food, but neglecting the weightier matters of justice and love for God (Luke 11:42). He condemned the practice of 'corban' (whereby a son could pledge his material possessions to God and thus duck his responsibilities to look after his ageing parents in a society with no welfare state) because it nullified the sixth commandment (Matthew 15:3–7).

In the parable of the Pharisee and tax collector (Luke 19:9–14) he taught that an honest heart was more important than the right form of words. And he told the rich young man to sell his possessions, to give to the poor and to follow him, because, although the young man kept the law, his worship was defiled by his lifestyle (Luke 18:18–30).

Jesus' view of worship was summed up in his conversation with a Samaritan woman at a well. What matters, he said, is not form or place but spirit and truth (John 4:19–24). The implication of this is that worship is a matter of lifestyle, of living the truth in a right relationship with God; an implication drawn out by Jesus' interest not in what the woman said at church but in her domestic arrangements.

So it must be for prayer?

If worship was a way of life, and not what the early church did when they met, what about prayer? Most people would put prayer near the top of their list of what the church is for. And yes, prayer was a central religious activity in the ancient world. People went to temples to join in the prayers led by priests and holy men. But the early Christians' experience of prayer was revolutionized by Jesus. You didn't need to go to a temple or church to pray. He prayed on the road, in the hills, wherever he was. He learned this pattern of praying from his Jewish upbringing, but he transformed it by the depth and vibrancy of his relationship with God, a God he always referred to (except in his dying moments on the cross) as Father.

It was the intimacy and familiarity of Jesus' relationship with God that so startled his first followers. They'd been brought up in a culture that referred to God by a number of euphemisms – the 'Name' or the 'Wisdom'. This probably accounts for Matthew's use of 'kingdom of heaven' to describe Jesus' agenda rather than Luke's and Mark's more direct 'kingdom of God'. God was a distant presence in formal first-century Judaism; he was a close confidante to Jesus, and his first disciples saw it. So they asked him to teach them to pray (Luke 11:1).

Jesus told his disciples to pray in his name; that is, to come to God, his Father, through him (John 13:13–14; 14:23–24). This was because Jesus had become the focus of God's saving activity in the world. This meant that for the early Christians Jesus replaced the temple. This had been foreshadowed in Jesus' ministry as he forgave sins (something a good Jew went to the temple for) and, most dramatically, in his 'cleansing of the temple', when, by turning over the moneychangers' tables and driving out the sacrificial animals, he was saying, 'I am about to replace this temple with my body as the place of forgiveness.' And so the New Testament writers understood that on the cross Jesus bore the sins of the world, and thus it was through Jesus and not through the temple that forgiveness of sins was possible.[4]

When the early Christians met together, then, they didn't

do so particularly to pray to God or to receive forgiveness for sins. All those things they received through Jesus and enjoyed at any time and in any place. They did not gather for religious reasons to do religious things. So why did they meet?

God's building project

According to Robert Banks, the church met to equip and build one another up to live lives of worship in the world. 'The purpose of church is the growth and edification [the building up] of its members into Christ and into a common life through their God-given ministry to each other (1 Corinthians 14:12, 19, 26).'[5]

Howard Marshall fleshes this out. Christian gatherings had a three-way movement, he says: God to people; people to God; person to person. 'The primary element is the God–man movement, downward rather than upward,' he says, 'in which God comes to his people and uses human servants to convey his salvation to them, to strengthen and upbuild them. He bestows gifts in order to equip the members of the church to serve one another.'[6]

This is the obvious point of Paul's teaching in 1 Corinthians 12 – 14. The Christians gathered together to build one another up in their faith, to strengthen, support and encourage one another for their lives in the world. This was a primary purpose of the spiritual gifts that Paul talks about in this passage.

Of course, this didn't just happen spontaneously; all churches need to be organized in some way. From the earliest New Testament times, churches had leaders and teachers, and people to handle the finances and to check that everyone was being looked after. Pretty soon it became clear that certain people within each group had a way with words and could teach the truths of the faith; others were particularly good at telling the story of Jesus to outsiders and persuading them to follow him; still others were generous with what God had given them and shared with those in need; and others seemed to be able to say something that at that very moment just summed things up and seemed to be the very word of God.

Paul in his letters referred to these various leanings as spiritual gifts (the Greek word is *charismata* – from which we get 'charismatic' – which is derived from the word *charis*, which means 'grace'). God gave these gifts to Christians to use when they were gathered together. Gifts such as teaching and prophecy were vital for building believers up in their faith – hence Paul's urgent advice to the church at Corinth to ask God to give the church those gifts rather than others (1 Corinthians 14), and his exhortation that space be found in the gathering of Christians for those gifts to be exercised, because they were vital for building up the spiritual strength of believers ahead of whatever lay in store for them in the coming few days.

But were the gifts given solely to be used when the church was gathered together? This is something we'll return to in chapter 8, where we shall be especially concerned to note what the New Testament says about the difference between spiritual gifts and natural abilities – if it says anything! Paul seems to suggest that it does not (but we're getting ahead of ourselves). The gift of tongues, a valuable ability to pray in a language you haven't learned – seems to be recommended mainly for private devotions (1 Corinthians 14:1–19) – though Paul didn't forbid its use in public (1 Corinthians 14:27–28). The gift of evangelism can't be for the church: it must be in the world that those with this gift communicate the good news about Jesus to those who haven't believed it yet. Gifts of mercy and helps would be as useful in everyday life as in the hour or so when church was meeting.

Spiritual gifts have always been controversial; read 1 Corinthians 12 – 14 if you don't believe me! It seems to me that this is partly because we lay such stress on using our gifts only when we are gathered together in church. This opens the way for rivalries and one-upmanship as we jockey for position and places of honour and power. But worse than that, it leads us to think that gathering together is the be-all and end-all of being a Christian. We focus all our energies on what we are going to do when the church is meeting, and we have very little energy left for living out our faith in the world. This is the opposite of Paul's emphasis in the New Testament.

Further, the gifts are controversial because we think they are for us, to bless us and to make us feel good. But Paul stresses that they are for others, to bless them, to build them up for their life of faith in the world.

The reason God gives gifts, according to 1 Corinthians 12 – 14, is so that the church might be strengthened. As we have seen, this means that Christians are encouraged and equipped for their lives of worship in the world throughout the week. The whole point of my bringing what I believe to be a prophecy to a meeting is that someone or some people will be helped, by what God says through me, to live more effectively for him on Monday. If that is not my intention, perhaps I'd better remain silent!

The gifts are not trophies by which we assess one another. They are tools that are useful only in so far as they contribute to the building up of believers for their lives of worship in the world. That, after all, is what the church is for. It is a feeding-station to nourish the followers of Jesus Christ. It is a builders' yard where lives are constructed that will point to Jesus through the working week. It is a place of nurture, support, help and sustenance for Christians seeking to live as Jesus did at home and work. It is a place where we learn of the mercies of God to us in Christ, and where, in wonder and adoration, we offer him our lives, lock, stock and barrel.

The gifts of teaching and prophecy are very important: that is how God speaks to his people. But Paul stresses also that people should not despise other, apparently less spectacular gifts, because God's people are also strengthened and equipped to serve him through people's simple acts of kindness, help and mercy.

Recent research from the USA suggests that people are more confused than ever about spiritual gifts. Barna Research found that among born-again adults, 85% had heard of spiritual gifts but 21% (up from 4% in 1995) did not believe they had a spiritual gift and a further 20% didn't know what their gift might be. Interestingly, when asked to identify spiritual gifts, respondents gave a wide range of attributes including a sense of humour, poetry, drawing, going to church, survival, observation and being a good person. Barna points out that none of these appear in the New Testament gift lists.[7]

However we understand spiritual gifts – whether (with Barna) we limit them to what's in the various New Testament lists or we take the New Testament lists as indicative of the kind of things the Spirit gives to Christians (this is the view I tend to) – now would be a good time to stop and think: 'what have I got to offer that will build up other Christians in their faith?' Whatever that is, that's my gift (that's certainly the thrust of what Paul means by gifts in 1 Corinthians 12 – 14). Am I using it? Where? How often? If I'm not using it, what's stopping me?

Is it enough of a mystery?

There is an aspect of the church's *raison d'être* that Paul hints at 1 Corinthians 14:22–25 and which the alternative-worship movement has realized that we need to pay close and careful attention to at this point. It is that when believers are gathered together, there is the very real possibility of encountering the mystery at the heart of the universe, God himself. And that if such an encounter doesn't take place, we've missed something vital.

The danger with our discussion so far is that it can lead to the view that Christian gatherings are just groups of mates meeting to gee one another up for another week out in the world. At the heart of our gathering, however, should be a consciousness of the presence of God. As John Drane puts it, a 'key element of the historic Christian faith' is 'that people find their true fulfilment not only as they relate to one another, but as they relate to God through one another'.[8] This suggests that our use of our gifts to build one another up should be focused on enabling one another to encounter the living and life-changing God.

And it is here that the alternative-worship movement has recaptured something that all churches need to relearn: namely, that we encounter God through all our senses and not merely through our intellect. There is a danger in traditional Protestantism that the focus is on preaching, knowledge, understanding and words to the exclusion of other ways of encountering God. For people who are more intuitive, less turned on by intellectual debate, this focus in church can leave them struggling. We need to feel, touch, sense, see, even smell our way to a full encounter with God. Hence the alternative-worship culture's use of images, movement, music, touch and video, often all at the same time, to help the worshipper to encounter something of the otherness, the mystery, of the God revealed in Jesus.

I was recently at a gathering of students and church leaders. We kicked off the day with corporate worship, led by two of our number, which consisted of watching slow-motion video images of street people and commuters in New York, while listening to Celtic instrumental music and hearing words that described encounters between people and God. This led into a time when all the participants moulded spheres from soft clay and laid them in the middle of the worship space to represent our prayers for particular people present with us for the day. Once we had laid our spheres we were invited to light candles as an indication that we were prepared to be light to our brothers and sisters and that we were asking God to enable those around us to be light to us through the day.

The worship lasted twenty minutes and was profoundly moving. I had already had a 'quiet time' that day (something I don't manage that early every day!). But in that time together I felt I had encountered God in a way I hadn't done for a very long time. And it was an experience that lingered and nourished my awareness of God not only through that day but over many days afterwards as well.

Drane argues convincingly that such gatherings are essential for two reasons in today's culture. The first is that they are one way for the church to emphasize one of its central doctrines: namely, the incarnation. God's having become flesh and dwelt among us, he says, gives value to the whole of our humanity and not just our minds – the part of us that traditional Protestant worship has focused on. Using the creative arts to bring us into the presence of God enacts the doctrine of the incarnation and helps us to experience afresh the reality of God's coming among us in Jesus, the carpenter from Nazareth.

The second is that we live in an increasingly visual culture. 'While the church continues to operate in a literary format, the majority of people are now operating within a visual format.'[9] This means that if we want people outside the church to encounter God through our meetings, there will have to be more show and less emphasis on talk alone as the means of revelation – hence Paul's hint at demonstration as well as declaration in 1 Corinthians 14:22–25.

But while such use of video, music, touch, sight and so on can be a very helpful way of enabling us to encounter God when we gather, it is also a very resource-intensive, expensive way of doing church. Not every congregation will be able to mount such gatherings. Not everyone struggling with their current congregation will be able to go off and set up an all-singing, all-dancing alternative-worship gathering. But very simple things can be done that are equally effective: for instance, playing music on a tape or CD, showing a single image on an overhead projector or even enlarged on a card if the space you're meeting in is small enough, watching a video clip in a home group, using candles to symbolize what it means for God to be light and for us to reflect his light to those around us, and telling stories to one another.[10]

And a healthy by-product of this is that gatherings that include these kinds of ideas can be planned and led by people who do not have speaking or teaching gifts or any of the skills associated with leading more traditional church services. Alternative-worship meetings need people whose gifts lie in the creative arts – painting, drawing, writing, playing music, dance, mime, even clowning. It's interesting to note that the first spiritual gift mentioned in the Bible is in Exodus 31:2–4: 'See, I have called by name Bezalel … and I have filled him with the spirit of God [footnote reading], with ability, intelligence, and knowledge in every kind of craft, to devise artistic designs …' He was the foreman on the project to build the tent of meeting and everything that was to go inside it, where the people of Israel would encounter the living God. Such gifts can be used today in the right setting to help all God's people to encounter him in fresh ways and to build them up for their life of faith in the world during the coming week. We'll come across examples of this in later chapters – including examples where ideas from the alternative-worship scene have been integrated into more traditional church meetings to excellent effect.

So, what do you come here for?

My friends Anthony, Geraldine and Chris all like to come to church, though they don't like the music much and certainly don't join in the singing. What do they come for? Anthony once said jokingly that he came for the food. The church we go to does do great food! Geraldine once said that without the prayers and support of people at church, she couldn't have faced a crisis at work that led to her sliding into a bout of depression. Chris was somewhat isolated, away from home in a strange city, finding it hard to make friends. Church offered him acceptance, love and a place where he mattered. People missed him if he wasn't around. They rang during the week to see if he was OK. They invited him round for meals.

'Oh!' people will object, 'this isn't church! This is a social club. You could get that from Age Concern or a local pub.' And perhaps that's partly true. But, of course, it's not the whole story. Anthony, Geraldine and Chris can all look back over their experience of church and say that they have met God in the welcome and help they received.

Geraldine knew next to nothing about the Christian faith when she started coming to the church because a friend invited her. She struggled to grasp what was going on half the time; the preaching and music were alien to her. But the help was just what she needed, and the help and faith, the support and the singing, were so intertwined that she seemed not to be able to take one without being infected by the other. Soon she was telling other people that God was real, that Jesus was helping her to cope with her depression, and that she could get through even bad days because she could pray and knew that others were praying for her. Church resourced her journey of developing faith. It was a social event and an encounter with God.

A couple of years after she started coming, she got baptized. At that service she talked of how she'd met Jesus in the welcome and support she'd received from his people and how she was now learning to live her life according to Jesus' agenda. She was also encouraging her friends and family to take a look at what Jesus was all about by coming to church.

Nowhere is the idea that church is a social event and an encounter with God more evident than in one of the church's core activities when it meets together: the aptly named celebration of holy communion.

A banquet for the dispossessed

Fellowship meals were important religious activities in the ancient world. When the early church met to eat, they shared the 'Lord's Supper', an echo of the last meal Jesus had with his close friends. The early Christians ate to remember the death of Jesus and to anticipate the day when they would sit down to feast with him again when he returned in glory. Meals played a prominent part in Jesus' life and ministry. They were events during which he delivered a lot of his teaching, told great stories and indicated, by the people he ate with, the kind of people God's kingdom was for. The company he kept appalled many religious people of Jesus' day, but he was keen to demonstrate by more than mere words that the poor, the sinners, the marginalized and the neglected were welcome in his circle of friends.

But Jesus' table fellowship pointed to even more than this. Isaiah 25:6–10 looks forward to the day when God would throw a lavish feast for his people on his holy mountain. By the first century, this had become strongly associated with the coming of the Messiah. When Jesus was eating with a group of Pharisees, one of them turned to him and said, 'Blessed is anyone who will eat bread in the kingdom of God!' (Luke 14:15). He was referring to this messianic banquet and suggesting that only the holy – people like him and Jesus – will get in. Jesus replied with a story that suggests the Pharisees will be at the back of the queue, behind prostitutes, tax collectors and other sinners. Ever the diplomat!

Jesus referred to this banquet in Luke's account of the Last Supper, where he said to his disciples, 'I have eagerly desired to eat this Passover with you before I suffer; for I tell you, I will not eat it until it is fulfilled in the kingdom of God' (Luke 22:15–16). Passing the wine around, he said, 'Take this and divide it among yourselves; for I tell you that from now on I will not drink of the fruit of the vine until the kingdom of

God comes' (verses 17–18). Paul had half an eye on this future feast when he said that taking the bread and wine is about proclaiming the Lord's death until he comes (1 Corinthians 11:26). And John saw a wedding reception at the end of history, a fantastic banquet to celebrate the marriage of heaven and earth (Revelation 21:2). It is an image of the coming of the Messiah that is hinted at in the Old Testament, but which Jesus made his own (see, for example, Luke 5:34–35).[11]

When the New Testament church gathered, then, they sang (as many of them had done in the synagogue) and they prayed, thanking God for his gift of salvation and forgiveness in Jesus. They ate together, and as they ate they remembered the cross of Jesus. But the prime focus of their meeting was to learn how to live more like Jesus in the world.

God's work in the world

It is vital to grasp the fact that church is for resourcing Christians to live in the world because, whether we like it or not, that's where we live. There is a danger to which ministers are especially prone (and I should know, I am one). It is that we judge people's faith in Jesus according to their commitment to church. We say people are growing in their faith because they come to two services on a Sunday, are active in their home group during the week and serve on a committee that helps to run this institution called church.

Now, don't get me wrong, all these things are important. But none is the measure of our growth as Christians. 'God so loved the world that he gave his only Son, so that everyone who believes in him may not perish but may come to church, run the toddler group and learn how to preach a sermon.' That is not what John 3:16 says, and certainly isn't what it means.

Being a Christian is about experiencing, and growing in, something the Bible calls 'eternal life'. This is the life of God, the life we were born to experience and to live to the full, but which sin prevents us from enjoying; the life that we are born into and grow in as we follow Jesus. It is about being caught up in what God is doing in the world. Jesus called this 'the kingdom of God' (we might paraphrase it as 'Jesus' new world order') which was arriving through his life and teaching. This new world order is about the rule of God over individuals and communities. It will come in its fullness when, as the Old Testament prophet Habakkuk said, 'the earth will be filled with the knowledge of the glory of the LORD, as the waters cover the sea' (Habakkuk 2:14).

To be a Christian is to say to God, 'I want to be a part of this.' That means that in our individual lives we seek to live as God wants us to, to live under his rule at home, at work, at play, wherever we are, whatever we're doing in God's world. And it means that we join with others who want to live similarly in God's world to help and encourage one another to live up to the vision.

Church is not the goal of Christian faith; the transformation of the world is. Church is not the end (or goal) of faith; it is a means to the end. To establish the church was not the purpose of Jesus' coming. He came to reconcile the world to God. As Paul says, 'For in him [Jesus] all the fullness of God was pleased to dwell, and through him God was pleased to reconcile to himself all things, whether on earth or in heaven, by making peace through the blood of his cross' (Colossians 1:19–20). God 'has made known to us the mystery of his will, according to his good pleasure that he set forth in Christ, as a plan for the fullness of time, to gather up all things in him [Christ], things in heaven and things on earth' (Ephesians 1:9–10).

The church, however, is the primary way that the story of what God is doing in the world gets told to the world. Both these passages go on to talk about how God is building the church through Christ to be the channel through which people hear about what God is up to. But how? Except for a tiny minority of the religiously inclined, people don't come to church. So how will they hear the story? By the church going to them.

The New Testament speaks of the gathered church and the scattered church. The gathered church is any group of Christians meeting together for teaching and mutual support. The scattered church is individual Christians, built up by meeting other Christians, living for Jesus in their homes, schools, workplaces, sports clubs, parliaments, offices of state, hospitals, whatever.

Jesus speaks of the gathered church when he talks of the people of God as a city set on a hill (Matthew 5:14–16). The church can do things individual Christians can't do on their own. Through pooling resources, the church in an area can set up a project to provide services for the homeless, the unem-ployed, those with mental-health problems, parents and toddlers, the elderly, and so on. In doing this the church is living out the theology of the incarnation just as it does when it uses all the creative gifts of its people to encounter God in its meetings. As the church acts in this way, people in the neighbourhood will look on and think, 'That's just what this area needs. I'll go and get involved', or 'I'll go and get some help.' And through contact with a project, some will encounter the mystery of the presence of God.

Jesus spoke of the scattered church when he likened his people to manure. 'You are the salt of the earth,' he said (Matthew 5:13). Now the thing about manure is that, left in a great big pile, all it does is smell; spread around, it brings nour-ishment to tired soil and causes things to grow. Christians are like manure, spread out in society, doing it good through what they say and how they live. In the same passage, however, Jesus warns that we might lose our saltiness and thus become useless to God's agenda. To avoid this, we need to be getting nour-ished, supported and built up by meeting other Christians in church.

Geraldine, having got caught up in what Jesus is doing in

the world by coming to church, where she found support in times of difficulty, now helps at a club for people with mental-health problems that meets in the church. She still struggles with depression, but with Jesus' help and the support of her friends at church, she can get alongside others with similar struggles.

Chris comes to church only on Sunday mornings. He gets along to one home group a month on average. His job is demanding – he's a caretaker on a housing estate – but it brings him into contact with lots of people who never come to church on Sunday. He's able to talk to them about what Jesus means to him, knowing that people he has seen on Sunday are praying for him. Maybe when he has finished work, he'll drop in on church friends for coffee or meet them at the pub, and they'll chat about their lives and how things are going, share a joke or two, and generally unwind. It's not as religious as doing a Bible study, but sometimes it's just as spiritual, and is exactly what we need in order to remind ourselves of the grace of God at work in the world at the end of a hard day.

Anthony has the church to thank for his growing ability to read *The Mirror* and thus to keep in touch with what's happening around the world. An adult literacy programme run by a church charity, staffed by Christians from a number of churches, and funded by government and private-sector money as well as the gifts of individual Christians, has helped to break down his sense of isolation. He can now read the council-tax demand, and doesn't get in such a panic when official-looking envelopes land on his doormat. In fact, he jokes about it at his home group, where he talks about how Jesus has helped him to cut down on his drinking. Having read something in that day's paper, he's likely to say, 'Surely there's something churches could do about lonely old people in the area.'

What is the church for? At its simplest, it is to help people like these – as well as everyone else – to live as Christians in the world. We'll return to some of the practicalities of how the church does this in chapter 4. But first, if that is what the church is for, what does the New Testament say that the church actually is? That is the subject of our next chapter.

3 Bringing the church into focus

The two men were standing close together in the lounge, an incongruous sight. Al: tall, dreadlocks, check trousers, baggy jumper and DMs; Ellie's father-in law: shorter, burgundy V-neck and tie over grey trousers. Outwardly, these two men, from different continents, different generations and different social classes, had nothing in common. But they were united in grief. Ellie had died a couple of days earlier, and her father-in-law was saying how moved he had been by the support the church had given to his son John at this most painful of times. Al simply replied that they were family.

There was no artifice in Al's grief or in his desire to support John, a fellow church member, now plunged into a sea of calamity and sorrow. These people were family as far as Al was concerned. So when they were in trouble, you dropped every-thing and went to do anything you could to help. Many others in the church felt and acted similarly.

On the Sunday after Ellie's death, there was nothing ordi-nary about our service. Dallas, leading our family service, began with an apology to visitors that the death of this young expectant mother would dominate the time we spent together that Sunday morning. Our singing was subdued; our prayers were long periods of silence punctuated by short pleas for

God to comfort and support John and baby Cameron; my sermon, as you already know, was a barely articulate attempt to fathom the presence of God in this cloying darkness.

Ellie's death had affected all of us. We loved her. Now, as we gathered for the first time since she had died, we sought comfort with one another. After the formal part of the service, many sat in twos and threes, holding one another. Not much was said, but a lot of tears were shed. No-one that Sunday morning came expecting answers to the problem of pain; we all just wanted to be together to grieve the loss of our sister, to seek the solace of our closeness with one another and, through that, perhaps to experience that 'The eternal God is [our] refuge, and underneath are the everlasting arms' (Deuteronomy 33:27, New International Version).

One observation I had made that morning was that at times like this we glimpse what really matters in a way that we don't when life is smooth and easy. And one of those things is that we should tell one another that we appreciate and care about them. So often, church life is full of petty squabbles and power games. Losing someone you love reminds you that there are more important things in life than what colour the carpet in the crèche room should be, or who gets to sit on the committee organizing the summer children's mission. That morning, lots of people were telling lots of other people that they loved them: people like Al and Ellie's father-in-law.

Before that, on the Thursday after Ellie died, many people had gathered at the church to absorb the shock of her death together. 'That was a very special time for many of us,' one member recalls. Whenever there is a death, it is natural for the family to gather to comfort, support and cry with one another. Just being together is important. What is natural for the human family was natural for our church family on that day.

Family is one of the potent New Testament images of church. If you asked the apostle Paul what the church is, somewhere in his first sentence would have been the word 'family'. Other words would also occur – such as 'household', 'building', 'body', 'community' – but 'family' was his favourite. In this chapter we're going to look at some pictures the New Testament uses to describe what the church is, and we're going to find out how those pictures might help Christians in the twenty-first century to understand the church and try to be it.

Perhaps 'family' was Paul's favourite picture of the church because it was the one he got from Jesus. Scholars have argued at length about whether Jesus intended to establish a church. Some have said that he came to renew Judaism, others that he came to usher in the end of the world, and others that he wanted to make a few suggestions about how we can live together in a more peaceful way. According to these scholars, Jesus certainly didn't intend to leave behind him a multi-national institution with millions of members worldwide.

Family life

All this misses the point, however. As we noted in the last chapter, Jesus did not come to establish the church in the sense that that was the ultimate goal of his mission. But he did call people to join a loose band of followers, and he used language drawn from family life to describe how this band should live together in the world. He taught us to call God 'Father', the head of a family; and to call one another brothers and sisters.

When the rich young man went away sad because he felt that the cost of following Jesus was just too high, Peter asserted: 'Look, we have left everything and followed you.'

Jesus replied, 'Truly I tell you, there is no one who has left house or brothers or sisters or mother or father or children or fields, for my sake and for the sake of the good news, who will not receive a hundredfold now in this age – houses, brothers and sisters, mothers and children, and fields, with persecutions – and in the age to come eternal life' (Mark 10:28–30).

This is a picture of security and belonging. Jesus is saying,

'Maybe you feel nervous about striking out and following me. Lots of people aren't doing it – like this rich and influential young man you've just seen walk away. But if you do, you won't be alone. You're joining a family who will be all the things a good human family is to each of its members.'

Paul picks up this theme at the end of Romans. Chapter 16 of the letter is a series of greetings, and we tend to skip over it. It's just a list of names, we say, and we don't know any of them. But in fact these verses are bursting with family language. This is not just a list of names to Paul. It is a series of heartfelt and intimate greetings to members of Paul's extended and scattered family.

He lists a number of church members as people he loves: 'Greet my beloved Epaenetus ... Greet Ampliatus, my beloved in the Lord ... and my beloved Stachys ... the beloved Persis ...' and so on (Romans 16:5, 8, 9, 12). These are not members of his human family; they are his work colleagues. They are other missionaries and church leaders who have worked alongside him in his mission to tell the world the story of Jesus. Now this is not the language we usually use about people we work with. Few of us describe our colleagues as 'beloved'! But Paul does, because they are more than work-mates; they are family.

But the nicest verse (and the one that has the closest echoes of Mark 10) is verse 13: 'Greet Rufus, chosen in the Lord; and greet his mother – a mother to me also.' Here is Paul – often seen as a bit of a cold fish who was a workaholic and ruthlessly logical thinker – greeting a woman who has mothered him. And clearly he is grateful for that mothering. She is someone from the family of God who has made Paul's life much more pleasant as he has worked to fulfil his calling from the Lord.

I have a mother in the Lord whom I think of every time I read this verse. I became a Christian in Audrey's front room (probably), because of her patient listening to my teenage ramblings and questioning (certainly). The wife of a full-time travelling evangelist, she helped me to grasp the basics of the Christian faith and she was there to listen when I found things difficult or puzzling. She made me cups of tea whenever I called, and opened her home to me and my friends. I am still very fond of her, over twenty-five years later. She is a special part of my family.

It isn't just Romans 16 that is full of family language. Everywhere in Paul's writing we come across it. For instance, Tychicus is described not merely as a colleague but as a beloved brother (Colossians 4:7); Philemon is not just a church leader, he is a brother (Philemon 7); Timothy is not just a fellow worker, he is a son (Philippians 2:22).

This language was more than just words. The family nature of the New Testament church was a reality that cut across racial and class lines. Paul, a Jew, was able to describe Gentiles as brothers and sisters (Romans 16:2; Philemon 7; Philippians 3:1). And Philemon, a rich slave-owner, could be urged on the basis of his faith to take back Onesimus, his runaway slave, as a brother (Philemon 15–16). The implication of Paul's plea to Philemon was that the two men, divided by class and wealth, would live together as family under the Philemon's roof.

This is most strongly seen in Paul's letter to the Galatian church, where he stresses that our unity in Christ is more important than ethnic, racial or class divisions. In that letter he relates how he had challenged Peter, one of the key leaders of the early church, because Peter had not treated Gentile Christians in the same way that he treated Jewish ones. Paul says this is a scandal, a denial of the work of Jesus on the cross, a rejection of the gospel of grace whereby our relationship with God depends on faith in Christ and not our religious preferences. Paul goes on to argue fiercely with those who make Gentile members of the family of Christ behave as though they were Jewish, forcing them to live according to Jewish customs. Rather, says Paul, through our faith in Jesus alone we become members of his family and thus we should treat anyone who names the name of Jesus as our brother or sister regardless of their race, class, gender and the branch of the Christian church they belong to (Galatians 3:28). This letter needs to be heard more frequently in today's church.[1]

Blood is thicker ...

All this points to the fact that the picture of the church as family is more than just an image. It describes reality. What happens when someone becomes a Christian is that he or she becomes a child of God (John 1:12). Indeed, Paul describes it in terms of becoming an heir to the estate. There is no suggestion that God is ever going to die, of course. The picture is of becoming a member of a family, who will share in all the good things that the family enjoys (Romans 8:14–17). We have become family members through the work of God's Spirit in our lives made possible by Jesus' death on the cross. As Paul describes it earlier in Romans, we are all separated from the family of God by our sin, but if we decide to follow Jesus and get involved in what he's doing in the world, then through his sacrifice our sins are washed away and we are welcomed into God's family (Romans 3:21–26). We become members by faith, not by religious observance, as we have seen Paul stress in Galatians.

The apostle Peter talks of our being born again into a new life through Jesus. This new life involved our being 'ransomed', or bought out of an old way of life which Peter describes as empty and futile, by the blood of Jesus. And the point of being ransomed is that we become part of a new people or family of God (1 Peter 1 – 2). There is, then, a very real sense in which the New Testament understands Christians to be blood relatives, all brought into the family of God through the blood of Jesus. We are intimately and eternally related to each other. When we look around church on a Sunday morning, this fact might thrill or appal us, depending on which brothers and sisters our eyes alight on. But it's true none the less.

Of course, not all of us feel this. We maybe feel close to Jesus as our saviour and brother, but we feel distant from the people sitting next to us in church. The reason for this is that though something might be theologically true, we still have to work at making it a reality in our lives. Just because I am related by blood to every Christian everywhere in the world, it doesn't mean I have a relationship with them. If I meet a Christian for the first time, I still have to go through the normal human process of getting to know them, finding out about their lives, what makes them tick, what their likes and dislikes are. I will more naturally hit it off with some Christians than with others. I confess that there are some Christians I find it hard to like, and hence to spend the time with them that I would need to spend in order to get to know them.

But because I am related to them through our common faith in Jesus, I have the basis for getting to know other Christians that I don't have in getting to know my non-Christian neighbours or work colleagues. At root we share something that is vital for both our lives – a faith in Jesus. This should form the basis of my willingness to persevere in relating to Christian brothers and sisters. And when I do that, I'm frequently surprised at how much I find I have in common with brothers and sisters I don't immediately hit it off with.

Being family obviously has implications about how we relate to one another. It certainly did for the early believers. One of the basic family texts of the New Testament is John 13:34–35: 'I give you a new commandment, that you love one another. Just as I have loved you, you also should love one another. By this everyone will know that you are my disciples, if you have love for one another.'

I have yet to meet a family that is all sweetness and light all the time. Our experience of family life is one of good times mixed with times of tension, arguments, disputes and rows. For many of us, our experience of family has been positive overall. We received encouragement, discipline and support as we were growing up; our parents are now our friends. For others of us, family has been a decidedly mixed blessing that has left scars into adulthood. Healing, or at least perspective, has come from putting as much distance between us and our parents as we can.

Whatever our experience of our human family, none of us should come to the picture of the church as family with expectations that it will be perfect. After all, we only have to look at Paul's row with Peter in Galatians 2, or his frosty relationship with James, or the grief that his relationship with the church at Corinth caused him to see that even in those heady early days, Christian family life was fraught with tension. What a look at Paul's life shows us, though, is that despite the difficulties, he didn't walk away from these relationships. It would have been so easy for him to dump the Corinthians and concentrate on a bunch of Christians who seemed to like him better.

I had a sharp disagreement one Sunday morning with Asif. He struggled with church, feeling that he was tolerated rather than welcomed. Extremely gifted, he'd offered to help with the young people, but had been snubbed, he felt, by the current leadership. I was available, so he tore into me, telling me a few home truths about the church's attitude to people from ethnic-minority communities. I was stung. I hit back with a few ill-chosen words about chips on shoulders. It was ugly. But it wasn't permanent. Because we actually believed that we were brothers, we were able to find common ground. Eventually we were able to see each other's point of view (albeit grudgingly at first); after which we were able to forgive each other for the stupid things each had said and engage in a constructive dialogue about Asif's involvement in church. The church not only got an able and energetic youth worker, but I got a friend – which was much more important.

Churches are collections of sinners, led by sinners, and they can be damaging places just like human families. But if we recognize that fact, and the fact that the New Testament picture gives us something to aim at, we'll find it a helpful picture as we think about how the church should function if it is to be a family.

A game of patience

The first implication of church as family grows directly out of this. It is that we need to have realistic expectations and be patient with one another. It is no accident that patience is part of the fruit that the Spirit grows in us (Galatians 5:22). It is not without reason that Paul tells us to 'Bear with one another and, if anyone has a complaint against another, forgive each other; just as the Lord has forgiven you, so you also must forgive' (Colossians 3:13), or 'Accept one another … just as Christ accepted you' (Romans 15:7, New International Version). Nor is it surprising that Peter appeals to his readers to 'have unity of spirit, sympathy, love for one another, a tender heart, and a humble mind. Do not repay evil for evil or abuse for abuse; but, on the contrary, repay with a blessing' (1 Peter 3:8–9).

Both these guys had enough experience of church as family to know that the path of Christian living is not always smooth. Writing to the Romans, Paul had to deal with a situation where some of the Christians, who were comfortable with eating meat bought in the market (and therefore sacrificed to idols in pagan temples), were looking down on other Christians who were uneasy about it. Paul probably sided with the meat-eaters. He calls them the strong ones. But he says that the strong must consider the scruples of those he calls the weak.

At the beginning of Romans 14, he says that we should welcome those who are 'weak' in the faith, but not so that we can pick a quarrel with them or take them aside for counselling or whatever euphemism we use for spiritual one-upmanship. I'm sure we've all had the experience of being

taken aside by well-meaning Christians and told that our faith
is defective and we ought to be more like them. Of course, it's
never put that way, not in so many words; but that is what's
meant. I have had it done to me over speaking in tongues (I
don't), over dancing in church (the rest of the congregation
would not be able to bear the hilarity or the distraction), and
over someone wanting me to wear shirt and tie when I come
to church, out of respect to God (Jesus didn't, so why should
I?).

Usually, the things that we want to quarrel about in church
don't really matter. After all, it didn't really matter whether you
ate meat in ancient Rome or gloried in a vegetarian diet. It
doesn't matter today – though I have heard of one group that
associates vegetarianism with demon possession (heaven help
them!). These days we often pick fights over music in church,
how and when to have a 'quiet time' or whatever we call our
personal devotions, and what we wear to meetings – things
that really don't matter. Sometimes we fall out over doctrines.
I was talking recently to a prominent evangelical leader. He
said he was finding it increasingly difficult to have fellowship
with other evangelicals who did not believe in the eternal
punishment of sinners or a literal six-day creation. Is this really
something we ought to be falling out over?

There are times when it is appropriate to challenge what
someone is saying or doing, as Paul did with Peter. But the
incident at Antioch described in Galatians 2 was not a row
about table manners, dressing for dinner or what was eaten as
the starter. Peter was eating with Gentile believers when there
were no Jewish believers around, but withdrawing as soon as
prominent people arrived from Jerusalem. Paul said that by
doing this, Peter brought the good news of Jesus into disrepute
and threatened the faith of impressionable younger Christians.

Paul and Peter both believed that people became Christians
through their faith in Jesus. But there was a powerful group of
Christians who believed that you also had to observe some of

the old Jewish practices, such as circumcision, keeping the sabbath and the dietary regulations – the so-called 'works of the law', the things that set the Jews apart from the rest of humankind. This group plainly exercised a hold over Peter. To some extent, Paul didn't mind if Peter still observed the Jewish dietary regulations – consenting adults in private, and all that. But if it prevented Peter from having genuine fellowship with other believers, and made those believers feel like second-class Christians, Paul was having none of it. In Christ we are all members of one family. So he challenged Peter publicly over the issue. From the content of Peter's later letters, it's clear that he benefited from it.[2]

The thing about the family of God is that we're all at different stages in our individual development. Some of us are infants, some entering adolescence, some grown up. Not surprisingly, therefore, we have different outlooks, changing opinions and vastly different needs, which means that we must be patient with one another and trust God rather more than we do to bring us all to the same place in the end.

The difficulty is that if we feel on the edge of things at church, we maybe don't feel we have enough of a relationship with anyone at church to quarrel with them. We might feel that it's not worth getting behind the front that Christians are often guilty of putting up. Asif thought it was worth it and I'm glad he did – though our relationship hasn't been all sweetness and light since that first row.

One of the complications of Christian relationships – and one reason, I suspect, why the New Testament stresses the need for patience and forgiveness – is that we find it hard to be ourselves when we're with other Christians. We have an image of what we think a Christian should be like – of what we think other Christians will expect us to be like – and we try to project that image when we're with other Christians. The problem is that makes us difficult to get to know. A friend of mine says she finds it easier to make friends with non-

Christians than with people in her church. I think the reason for this is that people in her church are on their guard, not wishing to be found wanting in their faith by her.

John possibly has this in mind when he says that 'perfect love casts out fear' (1 John 4:18). We often read this as being about our relationship with God. And it is true that through faith in Jesus we are freed from the fear of punishment because Jesus has borne our punishment for us on the cross. But everything John says about our relationship with God in this letter applies to our relationships with one another. So, for instance, he says that if we walk in the light with God we have fellowship with one another (1:7): our relationship with God directly affects our relationships with our fellow believers and *vice versa*. So where John says that 'perfect love casts out fear', this applies to my relationships with my brothers and sisters just as much as to my relationship with God. My love for my brothers and sisters – if it's for real – creates an atmosphere that is free from judgment.

So instead of Christians putting on a front for fear of being judged if their brothers and sisters saw the real them, we should be learning to be open and transparent, confident that our fellow Christians are not looking on us to judge us. This isn't easy and doesn't happen overnight. But 1 John is a good resource to help us cultivate an attitude to one another that is free from fear. And we can use this whether on the edge or at the heart of our church. But those of us at the heart of things should make the first move towards to such transparency with those on the margins.

A couple in our church were converted at a Billy Graham meeting. We rejoiced. They started coming along, got involved in a home group and grew in their faith. One day, a concerned church member came to me and said, 'Do you know that Brian and Cathy aren't married? What are you going to do about it?'

It was a dilemma. Brian and Cathy had been living

together for a number of years and had two children at primary school. I believe that God's norm is that we find our life partner, get married, set up home together and have children. But in our society it is quite acceptable to find a partner, and then to set up home and have children without getting married first or at all. What were we to do about Brian and Cathy? They had come to faith in middle age, and their lives were beginning to change under the gentle direction of the Holy Spirit. Should I now go in and say, 'Look, because you're not married, you should stop having sex, sleep in separate rooms and get married as soon as possible. In the meantime, you can't participate fully in the life of the church'? Or should I leave it to the Holy Spirit to prompt them in his own good time to consider their marital state? After all, if God showed us everything he expected of us on the day we started travelling with him, we'd be so weighed down we'd fall by the wayside pretty quickly.

Our church decided not to force the issue with Brian and Cathy. Some thought we were wrong, and that we were selling out the gospel and diluting the faith. Maybe they were right. But about a year after coming to faith, they came to me and said, 'Do you know we're not married?'

'Well, yes, I did,' I replied.

'We feel it's right to marry. Will you do it?'

Naturally I said yes. I believe our patience paid off. Going in with a heavy 'You must get married now' message too early might have broken their fragile hold on God at the start of their Christian life. God in his time revealed his will to them.

We all grow and develop at different rates. Part of being a family is to recognize that we'll always have people in our midst at different points in their Christian lives, and to accept them and be patient with them. And when we want to pass judgment on others, to take them on one side and sort their lives out, let's remember that we're not exactly perfect ourselves. While we might be able to spot the moral blemish in our brother's or sister's life, we're curiously blind to the messy stain in our own.

There is a balance to be struck here, and it is very difficult to set hard and fast rules. But too often the church has come across to newcomers – people struggling to get a handle on the faith – as a place where belonging is bound up with all kind of rules and regulations that fit as comfortably as a strait-jacket. Of course, our expectations of people's behaviour grow as their relationship with Jesus grows, and sometimes it is right to confront a brother or sister over their actions.

Jerry worked for his church in a day centre for the elderly. He was single and keen to be married, but there were no suitable women in the church. So he looked elsewhere. He met Peggy at a family party. She was a lively divorcee, very sympathetic to, and interested in, Jerry's faith and work. They started going out. Jerry moved in with her. His church knew nothing about it because he was very discreet. When a leader got wind of it, however, the matter came up at the deacons' meeting. Opinions were divided about what to do. Should he be sacked because this relationship was bringing the church into disrepute? That would have consequences for the day centre. Should he be disciplined in some way, to stress the church's disapproval of the course of action he'd taken, which, at his stage of growth in the Christian life, he should have known was wrong?

It was decided to pay him a visit. He didn't think his domestic relationships were any concern of the church. Peggy got stroppy and defensive. It ended unpleasantly. The church decided to bar Jerry from the communion table and from doing any teaching in the church while he continued to live with Peggy, and to offer him one-to-one Bible study with a leader to help him with his discipleship. He resigned, and he and Peggy moved away from the area. It was messy, but it was probably the kind of situation that faced Paul in Antioch over Peter.

We'll be there for you

The second implication of being a family is that we'll be there for one another. Family members eat and play together, stand by one another in times of difficulty and help one another out. Even when we're not under the same roof, family members keep in touch and assist one another when it's needed. The same ought to be true of churches. The early church depicted in Acts took Jesus' words about loving one another very seriously and in a very practical sense (Acts 2:41–47; 4:32–37). The reason for this is simple and is spelt out by John in his first letter. 'How does God's love abide in anyone who has the world's goods and sees a brother or sister in need and yet refuses help?' he asks. 'Little children, let us love, not in word or speech, but in truth and action' (1 John 3:17–18).

Paul devoted a good part of his ministry to what is called 'the collection'. He talks about it in a number of his letters. For example, 1 Corinthians 16 begins: 'Now concerning the collection for the saints …' He is not talking about the weekly offering that we have in our churches – though I'm sure we've all heard countless sermons to this effect; I've certainly preached a few! He is talking about the collection of money he was making among the churches he had planted in the Gentile world; money that he would take to Jerusalem and give to the Jewish church there to relieve poverty and hardship caused by the famine that was affecting Judea, Galilee, Samaria and the surrounding regions at the time.

The collection was more than a relief effort. For Paul, it was a potent symbol of the unity of the church. It was a clear message that loyalty to Jesus surmounted ethnic, racial and class divisions. In 2 Corinthians he devotes two chapters to the collection. He says that the Corinthian church excels in speech and knowledge, in hard work and love. So it ought also to excel in giving, which he describes as a grace (2 Corinthians 8:7).

Then, having reminded his readers that Jesus became poor so that we might be made rich through his grace, he spells out the reason for the collection, and for the Corinthians' generosity: equality. 'Our desire is not that others might be relieved while you are hard pressed,' he says, 'but that there might be equality. At the present time your plenty will supply what they need, so that in turn their plenty will supply what you need. Then there will be equality' (2 Corinthians 8:13–14, New International Version).

Twice Paul uses the word 'equality'. The Greek word (*isotēs*) means 'fair shares' or 'equal treatment'. In our day the word is associated with a particular political view that seeks to use the tax system to redistribute income from the rich to the poor. Paul's teaching does have political implications, but its primary thrust is that among the people of God there should be fair shares for all. This means that within a particular church family where someone has material need, other members will help to meet it. This will be done in various ways in different churches – but it needs to happen.

Of course, it doesn't apply just to money. It applies to all areas of need. In our church we have been trying to get a sharing scheme off the ground for ages (no-one said doing what God wants would be easy!). Under the scheme people say what they are prepared to share with others in the church. This then goes into a directory which every member has. A member in need looks in the directory and finds another member who can help. The directory lists equipment that members are prepared to share (such as lawnmowers, DIY gear or tools for car maintenance) or 'services' that members can provide for others. For instance, someone with computer skills might be prepared to help another member with word processing. Someone who is good at making clothes might be willing to help someone else mend or make an outfit. The idea is that members share freely, and the money saved – because we don't have to go to commercial hire firms or service providers – is given to church work or charity.

There is a danger, of course, that because we are generous, we'll be taken for a ride. Jesus was aware of that when he said, 'Give to all who ask of you; give and don't expect it back' (Luke 6:30, my paraphrase). It is better to be abused than to be tight-fisted; better to be taken for a ride than to turn our backs on genuine need. When we read about the rich young man who was told to sell what he had and give to the poor, we're quick to think of him as a special case. We say, 'Oh, he clearly had a problem with money.' But the text doesn't say that. The shock of the disciples, and their conversation with Jesus after the young man had gone, give the distinct impression that he wasn't as unusual as we like to think (see Luke 18:18–30).

Paul does imply that among Christians there needs to be a balance between taking responsibility for our own lives and being supported by the rest of the church. In Galatians 6:2 he says, 'Bear one another's burdens', and in 6:5, 'For all must carry their own loads.' But even here the stress is on doing what is right (verse 9), which he sums up in the words: 'let us work for the good of all, and especially for those of the family of faith' (6:10).

Praying for one another

A third implication of being a family, which grows out of the second, is that we will pray for one another. In the last chapter we saw that this was one of the key reasons the first Christians met together. The New Testament is full of reasons to pray for each other. Here are just a few of them.

In the opening section of his letter to the church at Philippi, Paul expresses his total confidence in God (Philippians 1:6) and goes on to say that he's praying that each member of the church will grow in love, knowledge of the truth and insight into what's important, 'to help you to determine what is best, so that in the day of Christ you may be pure and blameless' (1:10). When was the last time we prayed that prayer for the person we sit next to in church? In verse 19, Paul asks the Philippians to pray for him, that he may be released from prison. We tend to think of Paul as a 'super-saint', but he was only too well aware of his need for the support of his Christian family, especially their prayers. In Ephesians 6:19–20, having urged the Christians to pray at all times, he says, 'Pray also for me … Pray that I may declare [the gospel] boldly.'

In Colossians 4:12, Paul tells us about Epaphras. He came from Colossae and was deeply and passionately concerned that the church there should grow in love and depth. 'He is always wrestling in his prayers on your behalf,' says Paul, 'so that you may stand mature and fully assured in everything that God wills.' Prayer isn't easy. It is a struggle to concentrate in all the distractions and busyness of our lives. There are people who tell us it doesn't work and isn't important. Paul holds Epaphras up as a model for us to follow.

The early church prayed when it was in trouble, when it needed guidance and when its people were sick. James reminds us that we are all prone to sin and so we should pray for one another, confessing our sins to one another (5:16). I'd add that we should pray with one another about the things that lead us into sin, the temptations we face at work and home and in our leisure activities. The New Testament never tells us to withdraw from the world, but it stresses that without the prayers of our family, we shall struggle to live as God wants us to in the world.

And if we need any evidence of the vital part the prayers of others play in our life, we need only look at the experience of Jesus. On the evening before his crucifixion, he took his three closest friends with him deep into the garden of Gethsemane to pray. He wasn't giving lessons that night. He could barely string his words into sentences. He wrestled with fear and doubt and other demons, and he implored his friends to pray with him. But they were tired. It was late. They'd eaten well and were dozy. After pouring out his anguish to God, Jesus found them asleep. 'Simon, are you asleep? Could you not keep awake one hour?' (Mark 14:37). There was agony in his voice. The one who would deny him before the world in just a few hours denied him his prayerful support in his hour of deepest need.

Do we pray for one another?

Household, temple, body

The trouble with 'family' as a picture of the church is that we bring to it the understanding of family we've got from our culture. In the West, family has come to mean mum, dad and 1.4 children. To people from Africa and Asia, southern Europe and Latin America, this is a complete travesty of what family really is. Their understanding of family is more like the New Testament's: three or four generations living under the same roof, with other relatives very close by. The New Testament picture of family merges with that of the household to make this point.

In Ephesians 2, Paul says that we are God's household. The household was the basic economic unit of the ancient world. It was where the family lived and worked. But the average household, familiar to the Ephesians, would have been a pretty mixed bag. The family would consist of three or four generations living together, farming a plot of land nearby or earning their living through trade or manufacture. Any manufacturing was done within the confines of the household. The residents would include not only family members but also slaves. Here then was a small community – perhaps as many as thirty people in some houses – living and working together, bound together in close mutual relationship, each one dependent to differing degrees on the others. It was a marvellous picture of the church.

The fact that everyone in the ancient world lived in a

household of one sort or another explains why so much teaching is directed at households. The so-called 'household codes' crop up in Ephesians, Colossians and 1 Peter, with teaching relevant to the organization of the household along Christian lines coming in other letters, especially Titus and Philemon.

The 'household' image merges into the picture of the church as a house or dwelling-place of God. Jesus had replaced the temple as the place where atonement for sin was made and where God's forgiveness was found. So Christians did not need a temple to go to. But Christians too are spoken of as being a temple. Peter says that we are living stones being built into a holy house to offer spiritual sacrifices (1 Peter 2:1–10), and Paul says that we are temples of the Holy Spirit. In 1 Corinthians 3:16 he applies this image to the church, and in 1 Corinthians 6:19 he uses it of the individual Christian, thus wonderfully capturing the balance between the individual and corporate realities of the Christian faith. The Holy Spirit lives in us as individuals, and we have access to God and communion with him wherever we are. When we gather together and build one another up in our faith (an image itself taken from the construction of houses), the Holy Spirit lives there too. Indeed, in 1 Corinthians 3:9, Paul describes the church as God's building project. The church is a huge building site. No wonder it can be a messy place at times!

Everyone's welcome

Probably everyone's favourite Pauline picture of the church is that of the body. It is not Paul's favourite, as we've seen, though he does use it in four of his letters (Romans, 1 Corinthians, Ephesians and Colossians). He describes the church as the body of Christ and Christians as members of it. He spells out what this picture means in 1 Corinthians 12.

Sermons on this passage often major on the theme of unity. Preachers focus on the fact that the human body is a unity despite having so many different bits, and call us to work for unity and to strive to live together in peace and harmony. Preachers who want to deliver this crucial message should instead choose Psalm 133, or the opening verses of Ephesians 4, or even 1 Corinthians 1 – 4 as their text.

1 Corinthians 12 is not about unity; Paul takes that as read, having spent the first four chapters of this letter appealing for unity and showing what that unity is based on. This chapter is about diversity. It is saying that within the body of Christ there are all sorts of different people with all sorts of different gifts, abilities and callings, just as within the human body there are all sorts of bits and pieces – eyes, ears, feet, hands, kidneys, brain, and so on – that have different functions. And just as all the parts of the human body are needed and important, so that when one part doesn't function properly we describe that body as disabled, so each and every Christian is equally important and equally needed within the body of Christ.

Paul's argument does not really begin with the human body. It begins with God. There is diversity in the Godhead. He is revealed as Trinity: Father, Son and Holy Spirit (12:4–6). Because the Christian God is a unity in diversity, so his people on earth will be a unity of diverse people. The Trinity, as a model of community and co-operation, to some extent stands behind every New Testament picture of the church as the community of God's people. The point Paul wants to make is that unity does not mean uniformity. A united church is not one where every member is a clone of the minister or leader. Having established the unity in diversity of the Trinity, Paul goes on to show the same principle at work in the human body (verses 12–27).

The point is not to deliver a treatise on the theology of God, still less to give a basic biology lesson. The point is about gifts. Gifts are a sign of diversity, given to help to build a unity of co-operation and creativity within the body of Christ. It is precisely because we are not all the same and don't all have the same gifts, says Paul, that we can grow as Christian people in God's world as we meet together, share our experiences and build one another up in our faith (the theme of 1 Corinthians 14). The tragedy is that so many churches force people into a particular mould, saying, in effect, 'If you want to feel welcome here, you've got to be like us.' This is the opposite of the open, diverse community that Paul was describing in 1 Corinthians 12.

This picture of the diversity of the church is something that those struggling to find a place within their local congregation need to see and hear. Those on the edge often feel that everyone happily at the heart of things looks and acts the same. 'I'm not really like them,' Dawn told me, commenting on the people she'd encountered last time she went to church. 'They all seemed to laugh at the same things, shop at the same clothes store, get moved by the same things. I felt like such an outsider.' Yet Dawn had found faith while away at university, and was keen to find a church now that she'd got a job in a town away from where she'd studied.

It would help if churches gave some thought to who gets a chance to say things from the front. If everyone on the platform is white, middle-class, middle-aged, educated and smartly dressed, it suggests that diversity is not really tolerated in this fellowship. People like Dawn will struggle. It would also help if people in the church were on the look-out for Dawn and could draw her into the kinds of conversations with people who look superficially the same, so that she could see that under the surface there actually is quite a lot of diversity. No doubt if she hung around she would see how different the people in this church really were. But how long can we expect her to stay, feeling awkward and uncomfortable?

The trouble is that, without that kind of introduction to the fellowship, people like Dawn don't hang around. They don't get to experience life in the family, don't feel welcomed into an extended household, and aren't made to feel that they are stones that could be added to the temple under construction in this church. And that's a pity, because Dawn has got gifts most churches would give their eye-teeth for. Will she get the chance to use them? I hope so.

There are many more pictures of the church used in the New Testament, but the ones we've explored in this chapter are the key ones. They are also the ones that probably have most resonance in our culture. But though we've tried to be practical in our description of these images, they need to be fleshed out with examples of how they can become reality in our day and age. We also need to ask whether church is the kind of 'thing' that can answer the longings in our society for relationships, a sense of belonging, and community – a longing articulated in novels, plays, contemporary music, and conversations with friends and work colleagues; a longing that maybe fills our minds with the wish that it might be true. That's our theme in chapter 4.

4 Somewhere to call home

'The trouble with my church', says Jean, 'is that they aren't very tolerant of children.'

'My church is really good for young people and young marrieds,' says Max. 'It's great to see them all there on a Sunday morning. But sometimes I wish there'd be a little more attention paid to retired folk like me.'

'There doesn't seem to be any place in the church I go to for my style of worship,' says Femi. 'The people are friendly and the outreach programme is great, but I long to dance in church sometimes.'

Children, the balance between the ages, and musical tastes are just three of the issues that cause trouble in our churches. Others can be added: the difficulties women still face getting into leadership, the unequal balance between the races, the dissatisfaction felt by many young people at the irrelevance of church culture to their lives … the list is probably endless.

But these tensions don't have to lead to the alienation of people from church, or to the breaking up of the Christian family into churches each consisting of the same sort of people. There are ways of creating the family of faith that, as we saw in the previous chapter, was the New Testament ideal. In this chapter we explore a few possibilities.

It's important at the outset to stress that creating churches is not something best left to leaders and ministers. It is people who create churches. Everyone who comes to a church – from the minister to the newest attender – has a role in shaping what that church is like. Clearly those nearer the inner core of leadership have more of an influence – and more power to make their influence effective. But churches that fail to listen and respond to those on the outer edges will fail to become inclusive families along the lines outlined in the previous chapter and will thus fail to attract and keep people keen to explore life as a disciple of Jesus.

In with the outcasts

The church is heaving. It is the Sunday after the election. Bill Clinton is the USA's new President, and U2's Bono is worshipping in San Francisco. In the city that spawned flower power, the Jesus people and the gay-rights movement, Bono worships at Glide Memorial Methodist in the Tenderloin district. On this particular Sunday, the people of Glide are rejoicing.

U2's biographer Bill Flanagan says that the church was a sleepy affair until Cecil Williams arrived in the mid-1960s to be its pastor. He 'turned it into a church devoted to embracing society's outcasts, and over three decades has made it a jumping centre of worship and social action for sympathetic people from all levels of the community'.[1]

Bono says: 'It's amazing, the singing's great, there's queues round the block on Easter Sunday. It's just a happening, really alive place.'[2] On that particular Sunday, 1,200 worshippers were giving thanks for Clinton's victory. Bono, overcome with the excitement and the emotion of the day, recalls looking around and thinking what the election of a Democrat to the White House could mean for the people at Glide.

'I was thinking wow, if you're HIV, if you're a homosexual, if you're a member of the underclass or if you're a woman or if you're an artist – and that covers just about everybody in this church – this is no small thing,' he says. 'This is not like a middle-class home where people say, "Well, it's a new chance." There's nothing small about this! This was from "We don't exist" to "We do exist", you know? Whether the actual real impact of legislation on their lives will come into being, at least they know they are included.'[3]

Whether Bono was right about the Clinton years is for others to decide. But it seems to me that he put his finger on something important about the church. Peter, writing about the exciting things God was doing in Christ, said of the church: 'Once you were not a people, but now you are God's people' (1 Peter 2:10) – words echoed by Bono's '"We don't exist" to "We do exist"'. As Bono looked around Glide, he saw a family brought into being by common participation in church, just as Peter saw a family forming around Jesus Christ as people were being called out of darkness into his marvellous light.

Clinton himself had visited Glide the previous Mother's Day. Flanagan records that he 'later told associates that he felt sitting there as if he'd found the America he wanted to see – an all-inclusive America'.[4] When politicians talk of wanting a society more at ease with itself, where everyone has a place and is able to make a contribution, they are often tapping into a deep cultural well that was filled by the spring of the Christian faith, which has done so much to create our cultural norms.

Some will object to Glide's congregation and Bono's comments. 'These are not our sort of people,' they'll say. 'Church people are good, living wholesome lives and up-holding God's moral law. Church is no place for homosexuals and others whose lives fail to meet God's high standards.'

The trouble is that no-one's life meets God's high standards. The church is for sinners of whatever hue. The whole idea is that through the church we become aware of our failure to live the way God wants us to. But it's to be hoped that, also through the church, we learn that God loves us unconditionally; that because of the cross of Jesus we are accepted, whatever we're like; and that in the church we find welcome, friendship and the wherewithal to live a different kind of life.

Evangelicals, especially, often struggle with this notion. We feel that the church should be a community of the pure, and that it will be a light to the society around us only by living in a distinctive, God-ordered way. And, of course, there is some truth in this. But it is not the whole truth, and its effect can be to confront outsiders with an insurmountable barrier to entry into the church. Worse, it can bar them from contact with Jesus.

A glance at the life of Jesus gives a somewhat different picture. He kept terrible company. He consorted with prostitutes, political low life, gangsters, those the charismatic evangelicals of his day (the Pharisees) considered 'unclean'.

Out with the Pharisees

John Ortberg is the teaching pastor at Willow Creek, one of the largest churches in the US. He has pointed out that the Pharisees, for all their right belief about God and their moral lifestyle, were the least responsive to Jesus' words. 'His message was received with the greatest eagerness by those who came from the wrong side of all the values issues – prostitutes, the tax collectors, the religious half-breeds.' He goes on to suggest that the ironic result of the Pharisees' rightness in belief and practice was that they had become unable to love. They 'did not want the sick healed on the sabbath, did not want an adulterous woman to be forgiven, did not want sinners to share fellowship with righteous. They came to see people they were called to love as "the enemy".'[5]

This tragic situation is all too often repeated by people who are in some ways the Pharisees' spiritual heirs: the evangelical church. With our stress on having the truth about God and how he wants us to live, with the recent rediscovery of spiritual warfare and the increasing prevalence of combat language in our congregations, it is all too easy to see the world as the enemy, and church as our safe base camp from which we make occasional sorties into enemy territory. The trouble is that it also makes us distinctly uncomfortable when someone from that enemy territory strays into our buildings.

But it shouldn't and needn't be like this. People in our increasingly postmodern world are looking for secure relationships, a place of belonging from which they can explore what life is all about. The last decade of the twentieth century witnessed a heightened interest in spiritual issues. The fact that this interest has survived into the new century suggests that it was more than just a bout of premillennial tension. It is more likely to be a reaction to the hedonistic materialism of the 1980s. But whatever its cause, it is undeniably true that people are open to God in a way that gives Christians great opportunities to talk about their faith.

So we need to learn a key lesson from Jesus. He called people to follow him, and welcomed them into his circle of friends, whatever their background, whatever their beliefs, and whatever their lifestyle. Peter – a fisherman, working-class, rough and ready, not particularly well educated – sat next to Matthew, a tax collector and a religious enemy. Matthew sat next to Simon the Zealot, a radical nationalist who, this time last year, would have been more likely to slit Matthew's throat than to share a meal with him. None of these had to sit an entrance exam in sound doctrine to join the band of apostles. They merely had to say yes to Jesus' invitation to 'come and follow me'. Jesus wanted their company. Their lifestyles and attitudes, behaviour and way of relating to God and others would grow and develop out of sustained contact with Jesus, through being with him, listening to him, questioning him – probably quite heatedly disagreeing with him at times – and through watching him to see how he dealt with people of all kinds, how he spoke to them and how he reached out and touched the helpless and unholy.

Something was bound to rub off on them. Peter became a great leader of the church and one of its first theologians. Matthew might well have written the gospel that bears his name (though we don't know for sure). What happened to Simon? Did he become a great missionary somewhere in the Gentile world, or did he die fighting for the freedom of Israel in the revolt of AD 66? No-one knows. What we do know is that Jesus invited each of them to belong to his group, and that through belonging they had the opportunity to come to believe his message.

More than this. We know that Jesus sent them out into the towns and villages of Galilee to show other people what Jesus was about and to tell them about his new world order. And it's fairly clear from Luke's account of these incidents and what happens around them that these disciples were not super-saints. Indeed, it seems they had the flimsiest of grasps imaginable on Jesus' message. And yet he trusted them not to bring his whole mission into disrepute.[6]

Do you feel similarly trusted by your church? Or do you feel that you've got to have been attending for years before anyone will allow you to do anything in the life of the church, for fear that you will turn out to be unsound or to do things differently from how it's been up till now?

First we belong, then we believe

'Belonging precedes believing' became something of a slogan in my church when I was a pastor – for me at least. It was my way of explaining why we did the things we did in the order we did them. Then I came across the same phrase in a couple of books written by people far more knowledgeable about mission than I was. This made me think that I was probably thinking along the right lines.[7]

Maxine was a young mum who came to see me one day

when I was very new to pastoring. She was not a churchgoer, but felt she wanted to have her baby baptized as a way of marking her arrival in the world. Now, I am a Baptist, and we don't do anything with babies and water (we do dedications instead). I am also an evangelical, and part of me was reacting by thinking, 'She isn't one of us.' But I agreed to visit her at her home, where I discovered that she was a single parent whose partner came and went but would be involved in the service. 'Oh, great,' I thought, 'how do I get out of this one?' I am congenitally disposed to not upsetting people, so the answer was, I couldn't.

But I had to think through the implications of what I was doing. As a result I learned a crucial lesson about church. Maxine and her partner were conscious of wanting to do something to acknowledge their gratitude to God (whoever he/she was) for their baby. And, let's be honest, they wanted a social event they could invite all their friends to. Now, what if I agreed to their proposal? I would be talking to them about who God is and why it matters that we are aware of him in the big events in our lives. Then I would be saying to them that God was interested in them and wanted to welcome them into his family. I felt I could say all these things not only with a clear conscience but with a great deal of enthusiasm. So I did, both privately in their home and publicly in church.

Since then there have been a lot of Maxines. God has spoken to me through many of them, for which I am deeply grateful. But in the early days, members of my congregation would ask me why I did the dedication service for people like these. One dear and longstanding Christian lady, who'd been in the church longer than I'd been a Christian, buttonholed me after one such service. 'How can you ask me to promise my support to these mothers we might never see again,' she complained. 'You're asking me to make a promise I can't keep.'

I had a lot of sympathy for this view and told her that I could understand her point. 'But,' I said – there's always a 'but'

coming when pastors say they understand your complaint –
'what we did this morning was to say to this mum and her
child, "You are as welcome here as any of us." More than that,
we were saying, "We will help you keep the promises that you
have made to God."'

I explained that when I make the home visit to talk about
the service of dedication, I go through the meaning of the
words that the parent or parents will have to say. I check that
they are happy to say them, and warn them gently that the
effect of saying these words is to invite God to become
involved in their family. I also point out that when God is
invited to come, he invariably turns up.

I further explained to my church member that I visit the
home after the dedication service to see how everyone's getting
on. These visits are opportunities for me to talk about all sorts
of things, including the good news about Jesus. The dedication
service has become a bridge over which people have crossed
into the church and over which the church has crossed into
their homes. What we have been saying to these families is, 'You
belong here, because church is where everybody belongs,
because God so loved the world (that is, everybody) that he
gave his only Son to save it (that is, everybody).'

My church member was happy with that, especially when I
stressed that she didn't personally have to support every family
we dedicated. The promises we made as a church were corporate promises. We were saying that we would do everything we
could as a community of God's people to support this family.
One of the ways we did that was by offering Sunday groups
for children, where they could learn about Jesus and meet lots
of other kids like themselves. The parent or parents would also
get to meet a few people in the church and, through getting
to know them, would find the support that friendship gives us.
Our hope and prayer were that through offering these families a welcome, a sense of belonging to God's family, they
would come to believe in the things the church family held

dear – in God, and in Jesus, whom he sent, because to know them is to have life (John 17:3).

At the church's millennium party I danced with one such woman who had brought her baby daughter for dedication about six or seven years earlier. Since then, Tanya had had an on/off relationship with the church. But for the past two or three years she had been getting more involved. Her daughter had had a tough time at school, and a church member had been able to give Tanya really helpful advice on how to help her through it. As a result Tanya had joined that member's home group and been further helped by the prayers and support of the dozen or so in the group. Now she helps in the crèche and encourages her friends to come along. She's still with her partner, who still doesn't show much interest in coming to church. But, hey, one step at a time …

Open all hours

The conversation with my church member over dedications set me thinking afresh. If belonging precedes believing for families who come seeking a service to mark the birth of a child, what about other people who come into our church?

Michael had been in prison. Now he was a member of our Job Club. Job Clubs were a Government-inspired means of helping those without work to find it. At a Job Club, members get training in job-search skills as well as free access to paper, photocopying facilities, phones, stamps and newspapers. The Job Club in our church was run by a charity that we and other churches in the area had set up to work alongside the long-term unemployed. I was delighted to play host to the Job Club, and every time we had a fresh intake of members I would go along and welcome them to the church.

Michael was not a believer, and he struggled to find his feet once he'd come out of prison. The odds are stacked against ex-offenders in a labour market at any time, but especially a time of high unemployment. We talked often about all sorts of things. He was divorced and had a daughter who lived in the Midlands.

One day he came into the church obviously distressed. 'My little girl's been killed. Car crash. Just eighteen.'

We paid for him to go to the funeral. I spent time with him talking about his grief and loss, and how he might get his life together. I was pastor to this man who came to my church from Monday to Friday but didn't know how to pray. We were the only community he knew. He had a sense of belonging, albeit frail – a sense that at the Job Club were people who cared for him, who saw him not just as a jobless man who was a potential positive outcome for us, but as someone Jesus loved and wanted as a friend.

Eventually we lost touch with Michael. He found life too difficult to cope with. He dropped out and moved away, submerged in a sea of troubles. He belonged for a brief moment and we don't know if he ever believed.

There were lots of others like him. But there were a few, like Rose, who came to the Job Club and then to church, and rediscovered a faith they'd had as a child. The welcome, and the sense of belonging Rose felt, helped her to think through what she believed about God, life, home and family. Through her rediscovery of Jesus at the centre of her life, her partner found faith for the first time, and they got married and got stuck into church – not ours, but one nearer where they lived.

Another group of people who come into our church are those living in the community with various kinds of mental illness. We run a daycare project with our local psychiatric hospital, and up to fifty people drop in on a Monday, Tuesday or Wednesday afternoon to play games, drink tea and coffee, and chat. Three of the users have come along to a home group. One is currently attending church regularly on a Sunday morning. Others come from time to time. This is wonderful.

But equally wonderful is the fact that many feel that our

church is their church. When they talk about the day centre
they talk about 'going to church'. When I first heard this, I was
horrified. I said to myself, 'It isn't church. It's a daycare project.'
But I realized that to these people it was church. It was a place
where they were welcomed, taken seriously, listened to,
helped. It was a place where they could make friends, have a
laugh, let their hair down, a place that gave them a sense of
belonging to something. Out of that sense of belonging, many
have talked to church people about faith; many have started
the journey we're all on of getting to know God for ourselves.
And for them, it happens midweek. Well, as the apostle Paul
said, there's nothing sacred about Sunday (Galatians 4:10–11)!

There are increasing numbers of churches that are involved
in weekday ministries to various groups of people. Projects
range from parent and toddler groups to drop-in centres for
the homeless; from daycare work with the elderly to training-
courses for the unemployed; from youth clubs to adult
literacy; from arts and crafts and after-school clubs to debt
counselling and family-advice centres. The range of needs is
huge, and the church is terrifically well equipped to meet
them – often in partnership with other nearby churches. As
novelist and vicar Simon Parke says: 'On Sundays we celebrate
the resurrection. On Mondays we give it away.'[8]

Of course, merely having a project doesn't create a sense of
belonging in those who come along. Those involved in the
project have to be consciously aware that the reason for
opening the church's doors on Monday to the unemployed,
the mentally ill, single-parent families, elderly people, young
people, the lonely and those at a loose end is that Jesus loves
these people – maybe people who couldn't cope or be bothered with what we do on Sunday – just as much as he loves
us. We open the doors, make them tea, and offer them
welcome and what help we can in the hope that, through such
human contact, they will sense something of that divine love.

It is this marriage of Sundays with Mondays that is so vital.

As we saw in chapter 2, church on Sunday is meant to equip us for worship in the world on Monday. This, coupled with the idea that people can experience 'church' in a variety of places, makes us ask again – but this time at a more practical level – what is church for?

One thing church is undoubtedly for is to give us a sense of belonging. All the pictures used of church in the New Testament are images of belonging, security and safety. This is something we shall pick up again in the next chapter, when we look at whether being a Christian without belonging to a church is sensible or possible.

Sunday night, Monday morning

I'm writing this on a Sunday afternoon. I was at church this morning, and in many ways the service was a fairly standard affair. We sang songs, prayed and listened to a sermon; then we spent as much time again chatting with one another over tea and coffee. Similar things happen in churches up and down the land Sunday after Sunday. So what?

I'll be at work tomorrow, concentrating on whatever the business to hand is. But I will also be thinking of Gerry, Judy and Cliff, with whom I prayed this morning. Gerry's back problem has flared up again, making work very difficult. He is particularly busy at the moment because his company is coming to its year end. Judy is going to a concert with a friend midweek and hopes she'll have an opportunity to talk about her faith with her. Cliff is looking forward to a holiday, but has lots of loose ends to tie up at the office before he goes away. These are people whose lives I share Sunday by Sunday, and whose lives I affect Monday to Friday by praying for them and by being available when work's a pain and they need a friend to moan at and pray with.

This afternoon Peggy dropped in. She was agitated about a meeting at her church that had not turned out how she'd hoped. 'I believe God wants me there,' she said. 'But not getting our point across about the needs of families was a real blow.' We sympathize. Church is never perfect. Some churches are less perfect than others. Sometimes we've got to hang in there, find allies where we can, and pray that God will move mountains. Peggy has hung in with her less than perfect church for the best part of a decade and she's been able to do it because of support she's received from a small group within the church and a rather larger group of friends willing to chat and pray with her outside the church. We'll come back to this in the next chapter.

This morning, before we broke into groups to pray for one another (we don't always do this, but it's nice when we do), I looked at Steve leading our worship, dancing on the platform, and thought, 'Yeah. This is a really good place to be. This is what I need this morning before the demands of work tomorrow. I need to let God know how I feel about him.'

There are times when, as I contemplate the implications of what I was arguing in chapter 2, I think it would be better if church met in small groups in people's homes, and focused on praying for one another and doing some Bible study, with practical application of the text to our various daily lives. And I do think there's mileage in this. The current interest in cell churches is very welcome. In many ways it is a revival of ideas that were being promoted in the late 1970s by Australian Robert Banks, American Howard Snyder and Englishman David Prior about the church in the home.[9] But the ideas weren't original then. Prior's book *The Church in the Home* grew out of travels among the so-called 'base communities' in Latin America and elsewhere. Snyder drew on Methodist ideas of the class meeting, devoting a whole book to the radical nature of Wesley's views on the church.[10] Banks based his ideas on his reading of the social structure of the first-century church and his understanding of Paul's notions of community.[11]

With the trend in the UK and other industrialized

countries towards more weekend working – Sunday shopping, twenty-four-hour banking, more professional sport
throughout Saturday and Sunday, and so on – maybe home
churches, cell churches, small groups of Christians meeting at
various times for fellowship, study, prayer and support, suggest
one way forward. It is certainly one that all Christians should
be thinking seriously about.

Such churches are able to meet the need people feel for
depth and closeness of relationship. They are able to offer the
intimate fellowship that is impossible in a large crowd. They
are also excellent environments for nurturing faith, and for
helping people to grow in their understanding of who God
is, what he has done for us in Christ, and what it means to
follow Jesus in today's world. New Christians, or believers
struggling with questions and uncertainties, often feel
marginalized by the 'one size fits all' Sunday-morning
worship service. A more intimate, informal gathering where
relationships of trust can be nurtured can be of great benefit
to such people.

Helen was one such. She came to church but felt lost and
bewildered. She couldn't get a handle on what was going on
at all. The songs left her baffled, the notices made her feel like
an outsider, the sermons carried too much information for her
to process. She was all set to chuck it in when she was invited
to join a small group for people like her. A few met in Diane's
flat to chat about life, drink coffee and look at the Bible. Every
other week the group met, and over time Helen began to
grasp who Jesus was and why he was interested in her. She was
able to share the frustrations of her work and family life.
Looking back on the experience she said: 'What I liked, I
suppose, was the fact that I could be myself … No airs and
graces. If I said something daft no-one laughed at me. I felt I
belonged.' About a year after joining the group, Helen was
baptized and joined the church. She felt able to cope with
whatever happened on a Sunday morning. But the core of her

church life remains the small group where she can chat about anything and knows that these close friends will understand, support and pray for her.

Small neighbourhood-based groups can also be effective springboards to mission activity. But their usefulness should not be over-hyped. Christians have a habit of wanting to re-invent the wheel when it comes to creating vehicles for evangelism. For instance, they don't join the local tennis club, they encourage a cell group to hire some courts and invite their friends along for a tennis evening with a message. Sadly, the message this kind of activity gives is that Christians don't really want to rub shoulders with those outside the church except on their own terms. If we want to do mission and play tennis, we ought to join the local tennis club and ensure our Christian friends – probably those in our small group – are praying for us as we do so. Small groups facilitate mission through supporting whatever their members are doing out in the world.

Cell groups of this kind are dangerous for leaders, of course. They cannot be centrally organized or controlled. They cannot easily be created in the image of the strong minister or leadership team. They cannot be policed to ensure that they are delivering the party line on all issues. There is a risk that they will stray from sound doctrine and become eccentric, even heretical, in what they talk about. That is a serious concern that needs to be addressed by any church thinking of organizing itself along these lines. Freedom needs to be balanced in some way – though perhaps trusting the Holy Spirit and the Word of God is better than cloning all the home–church leaders in the pastor's image.

The cell–church bandwagon is still rolling, and sometimes church leaders look on it as the panacea that is going to reverse declining attendance and fire the church up for mission. I fear that a lot of ministers are setting themselves up for yet another disappointment. But cells do offer a way forward in helping those on the edge of church to find a family where they can explore what Jesus means to them and how they might follow him.

But this isn't the only way of doing it, and as I think of Steve jumping off the platform, clapping his hands over his head and leading us in the chorus 'Our God Reigns', I'm reminded there are things you can't do in a semi or a flat. I should point out that leaping off the platform is not an every-week occurrence at our church, but it was the natural thing to do this morning. I hope I'd have done the same if I'd been leading (though perhaps I'm a tad reserved …). But what did it have to do with what I'll be doing in the office tomorrow, or with what Danny will be doing at the site, or Mel in the playgroup? Everything.

Our whole lives should be offered to God in worship and in gratitude for what he has done for us in Jesus. As we saw in chapter 2, the purpose of Jesus' coming was not to establish the church but to save the world through dying on the cross. Our goal in offering our lives back to him must therefore be to help in the task of winning the world for our Lord. We do that by the way we work, play, shop, chat, drive, wash up, garden, and so on, through the week. So what are we doing singing songs for an hour or so in an oddly shaped building with an odd assortment of people?

We're getting stoked up for the week. Our lives are like a long car journey. Sunday meetings are like the motorway service areas we stop at on a long journey to take a break from the road and get refreshed, fed and watered. The point of stopping at a service station is not to fill the car with petrol or to eat a plate of over-priced, under-flavoured food from the take-away. The point is to make ourselves fit and ready for the next part of the journey.

And that is the point of church. Everything that happens on a Sunday morning should have the aim of getting us topped up for the coming week. How does this work?

Take a break

Well, first, coming along to a building set aside for 'worship' is a bit like breaking our journey at a complex set aside for refuelling cars and their occupants. Church is a filling station or service area. We gather with others, who are also on a journey, to get refreshed and refuelled. Of course, we can gather to do church in a family home, school or community hall – it's not compulsory to do it in a special ecclesiastical building.

Linda and the children and I often drive to France, which involves many hours on the tarmac heading south. Once we did 650 miles from Calais to the Ardèche in just over twelve hours, leaving Calais at 9:30pm and driving through the night. We broke the journey with half a dozen brief stops for strong black coffee and neck massage. It was pretty gruelling. By breakfast time I was skewing around like a drunk, barely able to keep my eyes open, and Linda had to take the wheel from me. On subsequent trips we have taken it at a more leisurely pace, stopping overnight, enjoying nice food in reasonable restaurants, and taking in some of the local colour in small towns on our journey through France. Each night we've looked at the map, planned the route for the next day's drive and sightseeing diversions, and worked out how long it will take to reach our final destination.

Church is a bit like this. Through the week we are so focused in on the task at hand – exams, deadlines, meetings, shopping, keeping house, running our businesses, looking after the kids – that we often lose sight of the point of it all. Then on Sunday we pitch up strung out and exhausted at church, and the music lifts us out of ourselves towards God. At least, it should do. Sometimes the music makes us cringe and wince as we sing banal words to jangly tunes that have all the artistic merit of a chewing-gum ad. But at its best, church music (old or new) shifts our attention from us to God. Writing to the Colossians, Paul tells his people to look up: '... If you have been raised with Christ,' he says, 'seek the things that are above, where Christ is, seated at the right hand of God. Set your minds on things that are above, not on things that are on earth, for you have died, and your life is hidden with Christ in God' (Colossians 3:1–3).

These are fantastic words. Once we were dead in our trespasses and sins, cut off from the life of God, and separated from all that we were born to enjoy but which the fall robbed us of. Now through Jesus we have been raised to new life, a life that is hidden with Christ in God, a life that nothing in the world can tarnish, affect or snatch from us, a life that will one day be revealed in all its glory when Jesus comes again. Hallelujah and hallelujah! The trouble is that, bent over the photocopier on a wet Wednesday, when the boss is crawling all over your back for results, and colleagues have let you down, and you've had a row with a close friend, and the bill on your car is twice the estimate, it's hard to have any awareness that your real life is hidden with Christ in God! We need Sunday – or a special time somewhere in the week – to give us back our sense of perspective.

So what we sing is important. It isn't enough to sing song after song that tells Jesus we love him – true and vital though that is. We need to be singing songs that remind us of the great truths of our Christian faith: songs that tell us again of the love God has for each of us, of the sacrifice Jesus made for us on the cross, of the life we can enjoy now in the power of the Holy Spirit. For as we sing that kind of song, or listen to poetry or music that contains the same truth, or look at pictures, or watch drama or dance that expresses these truths, so our hearts are made to feel, and our minds to think, how wonderful is the God we are involved with. As we step aside from our travels and pull into the service station, we should be helped to refocus on the nature of our journey, its destination and who it is we're travelling with. The singing and the liturgy ought to do this for us.

Sometimes, of course, it doesn't. We are confronted by the worship leader from hell: the one who chooses all the songs we hate and tells us to lift our hands as we sing that chorus for the seventh time; the one who intones the liturgy in a sonorous monotone with all the passion of someone reading the ingredients off the side of the breakfast-cereal packet; the one who constantly apologizes for not having had time to prepare, and who clearly has no idea what point this service is trying to make. All we can do is grin and bear this. Someone told me recently of a service she'd attended where the worship leader had insisted that everyone raise their hands during the singing of the next song. She had put hers firmly in her pockets. Then she moved to the back of the hall so as not to distract anyone else, opened her Bible, and spent the service alternately reading it and meditating on the banner at the back of her church.

Sometimes we aren't able to join in the singing because we've had a bad week, the ghosts of which constantly haunt our thinking. Or we're not on the worship leader's wavelength; it's not that he or she is doing anything wrong, it's just that it's not quite scratching where we're itching; we have to wriggle to make contact. At times like this it's good to just listen, soak up what's happening, focus on a few words that seem to resonate with where we're at, think about them and allow them to lead us into God's presence.

The point of the music, the singing, the liturgy and the refocusing of our minds is to make contact with God – to come into his presence and allow him a good chunk of time to do us good, and to fill us up with the good things from his table.

Get cleaned up

The second thing we often do when leaving the motorway and stopping at a service station is to clean the car. Motorways are filthy places. The windscreen gets splattered with dead bugs and muck from other vehicles' wheels, the bodywork gets coated in salt, and our pristine car looks bedraggled and sad. So we get it washed, or at least we get the windscreen cleaned, so we can see where we are going.

Through the week we pick up all kinds of muck in our lives: all the things we wish we hadn't done, the words we wish we could have taken back the moment they left out mouths, the attitudes we'd be embarrassed to own up to. Church is a carwash for the soul. As we come before the Lord in confession; as we hear words reminding us that whatever we've done, God longs to forgive us; as we are told that nothing can separate us from the love of God in Christ; so we can feel the weight of last week's sin lift from us and know that we can start the new week with a clean slate. It may be, of course, that we have done something hurtful to someone in the church and we need to put it right. Sunday is a good opportunity to do that.

We reminded ourselves in chapter 2 that we don't have to be in a special place to experience God's forgiveness. Whenever we fall, we can get straight up again, say 'sorry', know that God forgives us and move on. But sometimes it's good to do this in a more formal way with others. Listening to someone else say the words can make the experience more real for us.

Check where you're heading

Thirdly, breaking our journey is the time to remind ourselves where we are going and what is the best way of getting there. Motorway service stations sell all kinds of maps and route-planners (and isn't it amazing that no matter how many you buy, you never seem to have the right one with you in the car when you are lost?).

We come to church for route-planning advice. We need teaching. We need counsel. Again writing to the Colossian Christians, Paul says, 'Let the word of Christ dwell in you richly; teach and admonish one another in all wisdom' (3:16). We need to learn about God. There are many ways of doing this. We ought to read Christian books (you obviously do this, if you've got this far through this one) and participate in a small-group Bible study where we can help one another to apply the text to our daily lives and share our insights with one another in conversation.

But a crucial way of learning the Christian faith is through hearing the Word of God preached in church Sunday by Sunday. There is nothing like good, consecutive preaching for enriching the life of a Christian. This is fuel for the journey. This is the powerful resource we need, in order to work well, to be honest, to care for people, to speak the truth in love and to keep our eyes on the goal through our week at work and home. And this means that it is better to go to the same place to receive such teaching week after week, rather than moving around alighting on good preaching or famous preachers wherever it or they might be on a given Sunday in your town.

But we also learn from one another when we're chatting over a coffee after the service. How often the conversation comes round to how we understand something in the Bible and how we apply it to our lives! How often we help one another sort things out, without really knowing it, just through talking about our experience and understanding of our faith! Truly we need to let the word of Christ dwell in us richly. And these conversations are another reason we should be getting stuck into one church rather than several. Such conversations grow out of relationship. We'll return to this in chapter 6.

Get help

Fourthly, there are times when we make unscheduled stops by the roadside. They are usually occasioned by some unexpected noise from the front of the car, or a sudden and inexplicable loss of power when doing 80 miles an hour in the outside lane of the motorway. At times like these, as we root around amid the baffling array of coils, cables and lumps of metal under the bonnet, we wish we'd renewed our membership of the break-down service. It is a huge relief when roadside help arrives and someone with a bit of knowledge examines the engine, puts it right and waves us on our way.

On our Christian journey we often need roadside help. We are scrutinized, shot at, and under pressure to live by everyone else's code and not God's. We are cajoled into sin by those around us. So we need others to pray for us; not just in a general way – 'God bless Mummy, Daddy and all my friends, and make all the sick people well. Amen' – but in specific ways. That's why I was glad to pray with Gerry, Judy and Cliff this morning. Next Sunday I'll find out what happened to them during the week, and I hope we'll pray again. (I asked them to pray that I'd get this chapter finished; I trust their prayer will soon be answered.) The New Testament is peppered with appeals for prayer. For examples, see James 5:17; Philippians 1:3–6, 9–11 (when was the last time you prayed this prayer specifically for the person sitting next to you in church or home group?); and Ephesians 6:18–20 (Paul here seeks prayer for his work, which, at the time, was being undertaken in exceptionally trying circumstances).

Church ought to be the place where we take on fuel for the week ahead. It isn't easy being a Christian in today's world. The odds are stacked against us. We cannot survive with our faith intact at work, at home, or in our sports or leisure activity, without being refuelled for the week as often as possible.

When it's hard to cope

But there are those for whom church is not this refreshing, refuelling experience. If anything, it is draining and energy-sapping. What can we do? We can leave (something we'll address in the next chapter), or we can develop strategies to help us cope with our church as it is, and work to change it into something nearer the New Testament picture. Note that I said 'nearer the New Testament picture'; the idea is not that we attempt to create a church in our image!

One thing we need to keep in mind is that churches are entities in transition. They are very rarely the same for long periods of time. Like all human institutions, they change over time, adapting according to who's leading them and who's joined them. Sometimes we find church enervating for a few weeks, but then things move on and change, and suddenly, for no apparent reason, we find Sunday mornings refreshing again. Perhaps we've changed a little, amended our expectations, and worked through something personal. Perhaps the church has changed, got out of the rut it was in, and is doing something new. The point is not to write the whole thing off after a couple of bad Sundays.

But perhaps we've been finding church a struggle for some time, and it doesn't appear to be about to change. Like my friend Peggy, however, you really don't feel it's right to leave and find another one. She came looking for advice on how to cope with her church. 'It's so wearing,' she complained. 'Yet there are some great people there and we need each other. The children would find a move very unsettling; it wouldn't be fair on them. I don't really think God wants me to leave. He wants me to stick it out. But how?'

It's all too common a problem. What's to be done?

Coping strategies include finding people who feel as you do, and meeting with them to pray and study the Bible together. It is best to do this on evenings when the church programme is empty. It is also advisable to tell someone in the leadership of the church what you are doing and why. Most leaders will not feel threatened by news that Christians want to meet to pray for one another and study the Bible together. (Those who do feel threatened have problems more serious than a couple of difficult-to-please members!) It is also a good idea not to hold your meetings secretly behind closed doors.

Having decided to meet – for instance, specifically to pray for one another at work – tell others in the church what's happening and when. This conveys the message that you support what the church is doing already, and are complementing existing ministries with your own interests. And it allows others, whom you may not know about, to join you. That way, you widen the group working for constructive change within the church. When I was a minister, I was not at all threatened by this kind of thing, but I did feel slightly undermined when I got word of secret meetings – usually because, by the time they reached me, the reports had been grossly exaggerated into accounts of conspiracies by clandestine groups to overthrow the existing leadership! But I was only too pleased to hear of people wanting to get together to support each other in their Christian life. Furthermore, I was keen to hear from people who had ideas that would improve church for all of us; after all, I did not have a monopoly on creative thinking.

The other coping strategy is to concentrate on the things that matter: relationships. What happens on Sunday mornings in church is fairly marginal to our ability to lead a Christian life. In case you think this contradicts what's gone before in this chapter, let me explain. Sunday mornings ought to be a time of refreshing, renewal and refuelling for the week ahead. But they are not the be-all and end-all of what we do as a church. Other groups, which meet during the week, might be of more help in supporting our Christian life in the world; let's make the most of those. But often the most refreshing and invigorating times we have during the week are those single conversations, phone calls or meals we have with brothers and sisters. Even if worship was dire on Sunday, and you didn't get to talk to anyone you wanted to after the service – because either you or they couldn't get out fast enough – a meal with friends, a chat on the phone or a drink after work can refresh the weary soul.

In our church, we encourage people to be in and out of each other's homes, recognizing that we are able to support one another better if we know one another and the pressures we're under. Recently, I overheard a conversation at our church that went something like this:

'Are you recovering?'

'Sort of. This is the first day I've been out in over a week. And I'm feeling a little weak.'

'Is there anything you need? I'll be going shopping on Tuesday, and I'll be happy to pick up anything you want and drop it in on the way home.'

'That's really kind of you.'

And so it went on. (I won't bore you with the detailed shopping-list that ensued.) You get the point: church is a refreshing, renewing experience when we leave on Sunday lunchtime feeling good, encouraged, and set up for the week ahead. That takes place not just through stonking good singing, but also – and, I suspect, for many more people much more regularly – through conversations and assurances that people will be praying for us in the morning.

But what happens when we feel there's nothing left to cling to in our church, when our coping strategies fail, and we see no future at all in battling on? We'll tackle this painful state of affairs in the next chapter.

5 Me in my small corner

Jackie had left her church. She was still angry. We walked, after a lovely dinner, in the glow of a sun setting in tree-festooned mountains, the greens set ablaze by the brilliant, blood-red handprint spreading across the sky. And she was still angry. The light danced down the hillsides, painting meadow flowers with vivid colour, and irradiating the whole creation with vibrant life. And she was spitting blood. It had happened six months ago, and yet her body still tensed and her mouth narrowed as she talked about it.

'I'm amazed we stuck it so long. But we felt that it was our church, and we had to. In the end it happened very quickly – over the rota for the worship group, of all things.'

Her voice betrayed her fierce effort to keep her emotions under control. It didn't work. The dam burst, and amid oceans of tears the whole story spilled out: how her life had been made miserable, her job threatened and her health affected – all by the actions of various leaders in the church she used to attend – and how things had got much better since she left, though her anger was still like a volcano in its intensity.

The leaders at her church had initiated a consultation exercise. People involved in leading aspects of the church's life had been invited to make suggestions about how to make things better. No-one was particularly dissatisfied with the church as it was, but everyone had felt there was probably room for improvement. So people had duly met and made their suggestions. The leaders had not only rejected every one of them, but they had then accused those involved of being disloyal and of failing to support the leaders of the church in their God-given role.

Jackie had felt stunned. She and her friends had felt hurt and betrayed. 'It was so unjust,' she says. 'It was like they'd set us up to fall. They'd engineered the situation to make us look like trouble-makers. Eventually, the leaders imposed a rota for leading worship, regardless of our gifts and availability. And we said, "No way."'

Even allowing for the exaggeration that comes from fighting and losing, the tale was a grim one – and unfortunately not that rare. People can use church to play their power games and remain blissfully unaware of just how many are damaged along the way.

Jackie was determined not to join another church. But she was meeting a group of friends regularly to pray and talk and study the Bible, and recently they'd even shared bread and wine. She was finding it such a help. I gently suggested that she was going to a church; that this group, small and self-selecting though it was, functioned as a church should, and at the moment was possibly her best option. She hadn't thought of that, but said 'Thank you' anyway. A year or so later, she joined another church and is hanging in there, finding a role for herself as a member of the pastoral team.

Mike called. He'd moved away and not found a church. Well, he'd not been looking that hard. His wife wasn't keen, the new job was demanding and it was just another thing he didn't have time to fit in. And anyway, he was still reading his Bible and praying, though it was a struggle. But he wasn't happy. 'Something's wrong,' he complained. 'I feel so isolated. I've got no-one to talk to.' He asked for my advice on a range of things. We talked for a while, then I gave him the phone numbers and addresses of a few churches near where he'd moved to and said he'd find help there. Was I being unreasonable?

When Mary and Jim moved house, they finally had the excuse they needed to leave the church they'd struggled with for a while. One or two bad relationships had made going along a chore. But they didn't find anywhere else. Other churches they went to didn't compare favourably to the one they'd left. The worship was dull, or the teaching poor, or the building and people unfriendly. They stopped going altogether. The pastor of their previous church called from time to time, and assured them that if they needed anything, they could be in touch. When a problem arose, they got on the phone and he tried to help them through it. It wasn't ideal, but at least they weren't adrift alone when the storm broke.

Bill came to me at a conference to tell me how blessed he'd been by what I'd said and how he'd found my Bible readings over the past few days an inspiration. I knew something was coming. And sure enough, he hit me with: 'When is it right to leave a church? I've got to get out of mine but I want to make sure it's the right thing to do.' He was attending a big, trend-setting church, full of Christians his own age, boasting lively worship, good teaching, lots of activities, and plenty of support. 'It's crushing the life out of me,' he said over a beer later. 'I feel hemmed in by rules and expectations. I feel I've got to be something I'm not. If I ask questions in my home group, I sense I'm being pitied by the leaders and marked out as someone needing counselling. I feel I should leave. When's the right time to do it?'

Why bother with church at all?

The trouble with questions like these, of course, is that there's no right answer. It is sometimes right to leave your church, because for some reason it is preventing your growth and development as a Christian, and to go somewhere else. Sometimes it is right to stay put, ride out the difficulty, and grow in the process. And, of course, there are always two sides to a story. What would Bill's home-group leader have told me? How would others in his church have described life there? But what is noticeable is the number of people asking the question. At the same conference Bill was at, I had dozens of conversations with people who were dissatisfied with things in their church and were wondering whether I'd recommend that they leave to find another one. I began to wonder whether it was something I'd said!

Increasingly, however, people are not asking, 'When is it right to leave my church and find another one?' They are asking, 'When is it right to leave my church?' The subtext is, 'Why can't I just be a Christian? Why bother with church at all?' And the reason is not hard to see: increasing numbers find church culture irrelevant to their daily lives, and involvement in church seems to bring pain, not healing, as they clash with the expectations and personalities of the other members and the people in charge.

The traditional response to this question is simply not good enough. And fewer and fewer people buy it. It goes along the lines of saying that you can't describe yourself as a football fan if you don't go along and support your team. Likewise, you can't claim to be a Christian if you don't go to church. But church is not a spectator sport, and Jesus is not a superstar we go along to idolize from a distance. He is someone we have a relationship with. My salvation is through personal acceptance of his sacrificial death for me on the cross. The issue is: do I have to have a relationship with other people in order to have a relationship with Jesus? And the answer is much more complicated than we would like it to be.

The New Testament, of course, never asks the question. It assumes that if people become followers of Jesus, they become members of his family on earth, the church. This is not to say that if the New Testament's writers surfaced in our society in the twenty-first century, they would equate what we call 'church' with what they were involved in (as we hinted at in chapter 2). The question about whether you have to go to church as a Christian, however, is one that can be asked only in a culture that sets greater store by the individual than the group. Our culture idolizes individual choice and freedom. The New Testament does not.

The western world's near-obsession with individual freedom, rights and choice is the product of the Enlightenment, not of the Bible. This is not to say that the Bible does not talk a lot about the individual and his or her relationship with God; it does. It is, as ever, a question of balance. The 1980s were the 'me decade', the decade of 'There's no such thing as society, so do your own thing with a vengeance.'; Everyone looked out for Number One and made decisions entirely on the basis of self-interest – enlightened or otherwise. It was based economically on a minor misreading of Adam Smith's notion of the invisible hand of the market ensuring that everyone would pursue his or her own self-interest and that this would work for the common good. Smith, the founder of modern economics, was presupposing a society run on shared values, mainly Christian ones, writing as he was in the mid-eighteenth century. That was not true of the 1980s – hence the level of damage done. This is, of course, a slight caricature; but you get my point.

Bubbling below the surface of the 'me decade' was a deeper, longer-term trend in our culture that glories in the name 'postmodernism'. This is a way of looking at the world that is in the process of replacing the 'modern', Enlightenment worldview. In fact 'postmodernism' isn't really a philosophy as such, it's more a mood, a feeling that displays impatience with being told what to do. One of its key features is the elevation of individual choice and freedom to the status of unquestioned shibboleth.

To the postmodern, the only story that matters is my story. The big stories that have been told to help us understand the world no longer amount to anything. Science, history and religion all become matters of personal preference. There is no truth, except the truth as I see it. And if you see a different truth, well, that's great for you and I hope you'll be very happy together; but I don't have to accept it or amend my truth accordingly.[1]

It is in this sort of climate that the question 'Do I have to go to church if I'm a Christian?' is being asked. To answer it and see how that answer might apply in such a climate, we need to look at how the New Testament understood individuals, groups and their relationships, and see how what the New Testament says might apply to life today.

Solo survivors?

In his ground-breaking book *Cinderella with Amnesia*, Michael Griffiths reminds us that the New Testament letters were written to churches, not to individuals. Most of the time, when they used the word 'you', it was in the plural form. (In Greek, it is easy to distinguish between 'you' in the singular – the old English 'thou' – and 'you' in the plural.) We read the letters with our 'I in my small corner' glasses on at our peril.

For instance, Griffiths asks how often the word 'saint' (singular) appears in the New Testament. In its plural form, he says it appears sixty-one times. The singular appears just once, in Philippians 4:21, where Paul says, 'Greet every saint.' Turning to Ephesians, Griffiths says: 'How frequently we hear expositions of Paul's description of the Christian's armour in Ephesians 6 as a description of the individual, solitary Christian in his lonely, spiritual battle with Apollyon. The idea of a solitary Roman soldier going out all on his own to fight the wild Welsh, Picts, Germans and Franks is quite ludicrous! They would have made mincemeat out of him. The Romans were so effective because they developed to perfection the military art of corporate manoeuvre so that their huge oblong shields fitted together to make a great wall which their opponents were not able to break. It is perfectly clear in Greek, Chinese, Japanese or any decent language that the passage concerned is a plural passage containing plural verbs and pronouns.' [2]

When I first read this, nurtured as I had been in a Christianity that laid great stress on the Word of God preached and imbibed alone, through a daily quiet time, it was a revelation. What Griffiths was saying was that the church mattered. I couldn't live an effective Christian life on my own, cut off from other Christians, merrily going along in my own sweet way without reference to other believers. Of course, no-one ever said I could. But at the same time no-one ever really told me what the church was for. Griffiths helped to fill in the gaps.

I remember standing in the modern amphitheatre of the university church of Brunswick in Manchester, aware of the other people worshipping with me, and able to see their faces rather than just the backs of their necks. I found myself laughing out loud. It wasn't funny. The preacher wasn't cracking jokes; the worship leader's trousers hadn't fallen down. I was laughing for the sheer joy of being in church. It had never happened before, and it hasn't happened very often since – though it has happened. It was a defining moment. Having pondered Griffiths' arguments, I was now experiencing, I think for the first time, the joyful reality of 'the fellowship of believers'. I was laughing for joy because I realized in my heart what I had been wrestling with in my mind: God has given me all these people to help me live my life in the world. I am not alone. I do not have to make my way to the pearly gates as a solitary traveller, a sort of spiritual Ranulph Fiennes, pulling my sled solo through the spiritual wilderness, frost-bitten, existing on survival rations, with only an unreliable satellite link to an unseen mission control for company.

I was like the little boy who was having nightmares. His dad came to his bedside. After a cuddle, Dad suggested he snuggle down in his duvet and go back to sleep. But his son protested, 'I'm scared, Dad!'

'You don't have to be afraid, son,' his loving father replied. 'Jesus is with you.'

'I wish someone with skin could stay with me,' said the little boy.

I'm sure lots of us feel like that. Yes, it's a comfort to be able to pray. Yes, it's wonderful to know that Jesus will never leave us or desert us, and that he doesn't abandon us as orphans in the storm. But it's also great to have someone with skin there for us as well! And that's what I discovered the church to be on that evening in Brunswick: Jesus with skin.

That is how the New Testament describes the church. It tells us that it is the body of Jesus. It says that believers are 'in Christ'. It says that we are the temple of the Holy Spirit.

The one and the many

It is that last phrase that gives us the clue to how the New Testament understands the relationship between the individual and the group. In 1 Corinthians 3:16, Paul says, 'Do you not know that you are God's temple and that God's Spirit dwells in you?' This is one of those examples of Paul using a plural 'you'. God's Spirit *oikei en hymin*, 'dwells in you', he says. *Oikei* is related to the word for 'house' or 'temple', and so there's the thought here that the church, the body of believers at Corinth, is the house of God, indwelt by the Spirit of God. Paul is talking about the need for unity in the church. A few verses earlier he had told his readers, a group of people riven by rivalries over gifts, styles and personalities, that they were God's building (verse 9). A better way to render that phrase might be 'God's building project', because in the word Paul uses there is a sense of something under construction. God's not finished with us yet – mercifully. Now Paul is saying that we should do nothing to stand in the way of God's building his temple. Indeed, we should all play our part in seeing the superstructure rise. In chapters 12 – 14 he explains how we can do that through the use of the various gifts and abilities God's Spirit gives each of us. Here he reminds us that the church ('you', plural) is the dwelling-place of God's Spirit, and we really should co-operate with him in building the church rather than doing it down.

In 1 Corinthians 6:19, by contrast, Paul says: '… do you not know that your body is a temple of the Holy Spirit within you, which you have from God …?' Here, though the 'you' is plural, the context makes it obvious that it has a singular meaning; it applies to each individual church member who hears the letter read. Paul is talking about a person whose conduct leaves a great deal to be desired and is bringing the name of Christ into disrepute among those outside the church. He is staggered that the church doesn't seem to be batting an eyelid about it. Indeed, some believers are even boasting about it, marvelling at this individual's freedom in Jesus. It appears that the person concerned is enjoying plenty of extramarital sex. It isn't on, says Paul, not only because of the misleading impression of the faith it gives to outsiders, but also because of the relationship between the individual and Jesus. Having sex outside marriage is like forcing Jesus to have sex with a prostitute, he says. This is because each individual believer is united to Jesus through the Holy Spirit's indwelling of each believer's body. So we ought to glorify God with and through our bodies; that is to say, in the way we behave in church and in the world.

In the space of a couple of chapters, then, we have Paul talking about God's Holy Spirit living in the body of believers. In the first instance, he is referring to the church. In the second, he is referring to each individual believer. This is because the New Testament sees the individual and the group as equally important and intimately related. The individual needs the group, and the group is made up of individuals all playing their part within it.

The notion of the isolated individual having any worthwhile life outside the group would have been a very strange one to a first-century Christian. Everyone lived in families or households. No-one lived alone. This is a curious notion in a society where increasing numbers of people are choosing to live alone. Recent figures from the British Government suggest that four out of every ten women are choosing to live by themselves. Similar numbers of men are doing the same. This would have been an unthinkable state of affairs in first-century society, and a puzzle to biblical writers.

Right at the beginning of the Bible, God said that it wasn't good for 'the man' to be alone, and so he created woman to be a partner, companion, and fellow worker. The narrative is often used as an illustration for marriage. There's no harm in that, but it is actually saying something much more fundamental: namely, that we are made for fellowship with other human beings. Psalm 68, which speaks of God's goodness in providing for his people's needs, says that he 'sets the lonely in families' (verse 6, New International Version). Life can be pretty tough when we're on our own, facing its ups and downs alone. God has given us structures to help us cope, and one of the families in which God sets the lonely is the church.

On his travels in the American Bible belt, recorded in his book *In God's Country*, Douglas Kennedy met Shirley. A big and beefy tomboy, she'd been a roadie in a band and was now part of the Christian music scene in Nashville. She told Kennedy about her arrival in country music's capital city. 'Like I'd just arrived … and didn't really know too many people, and I was doing eight-hour shifts in this real terrible restaurant and really hating the work. So, I was, like, unhappy – especially since I hadn't really found a local church which I was comfortable in. I mean, having a church you can really connect with is kinda like a crucial thing if you're a Christian.

So I kinda felt messed up for a long time and, I think, that's one of the reasons why I got into a couple of relationships where I really went way off course for a while.'[3]

There are lots of Shirleys around. When I left Manchester to start work in London, I became one of them for a while. I'd been heavily involved in the Christian Union and a good local church in Manchester. I had a lot of friends and a good network of support. I came to London, where I knew few people, and, having spent a couple of nights on the floor of a flat belonging to a member of a church pastored by an acquaintance, I found a room in a house with three strangers on the other side of town. I was a rather shy twenty-two-year-old starting a new job in a strange city, and, like Shirley, I made a few dodgy moves before I located a church and began to make friends. I nearly lost my hold on Jesus altogether.

Shirley's life took an upward turn when she found 'a real nice Baptist Church, full of good people who, once I started getting to know them, were real supportive to me, really helped me to get through the problems I was having'.[4] So did mine. Most of the people in the church I pitched up at didn't know I was having any problems. They just recognized that I was new in town and they made a fuss of me, inviting me for meals and to parties, including me in activities they were involved in, and making me feel welcome and at home. Without them I might not have made it as a Christian. I might just have drifted into a lifestyle that squeezed Jesus out because I had no support network helping me to maintain my relationship with him. After all, the pressure at work and the pressure at home – in a house full of happy pagans – would have naturally led me that way. And I, not wanting to be any more isolated and alone than was necessary, was, for a while, buckling under that pressure.

Church is important because in God's scheme of things we were not made to be alone. We were made for family, for community. Each of us individually chooses whether or not we'll follow Jesus. But our 'yes' to his call is a 'yes' to join others who are following him, so that we make the journey together.

But why church? Why not a select band of Christian friends that I meet and pray with from time to time?

God's rainbow people

So, here I am sitting on the front row – punishment for taking part in the service, I guess – and Alex invites us to get into pairs and share our picture of God. Her instructions are simple enough; it's doing it that's the problem. One attribute of God that's been special to you this week? A place that speaks to you of God? A colour that reminds you of God? Something God has done? No-one's sitting next to me, so I get up and look for someone without a partner. There's a hubbub of conversation around the church already, people talking, smiling, laughing; black and white, young and old, children and adults, all sharing their thoughts.

Alex calls us to order and people shout out their impressions. We create a jigsaw of God's attributes and our thoughts and feelings about him and what he's done for us. All sorts of things are shared; things I'd never have thought of. People from Africa, old Londoners, children, a thirtysomething social worker whose clients are mainly people with learning difficulties, a fiftysomething teacher – a whole range of people I wouldn't meet anywhere else – introduce me to thoughts and insights about God I would never have arrived at unaided. After the service, over tea and coffee, I chat with a range of people from at least three continents, people who are my friends all because we share the same space on a Sunday morning and worship the same God.

Why can't I just make do with a group of praying friends? Because I would rob myself of one of the key ways God uses to teach me about himself: the sheer diversity of the church.

One of the great things about the church is that it isn't

self-selecting. We don't choose who comes to our church. Everyone is welcome. The church is a mixture of ages, races, colours, economic circumstances, life experiences – a rich, diverse melting-pot of individuals made in the image of God, being built into a wonderful temple that will reflect his character to the surrounding neighbourhood.

The world divides us by class, race, sex, wealth and religion. Our news headlines are full of the consequences of this in terms of ethnic hatred, wars, genocide, suffering, horror – a deep and bloody fissure in the world's body politic. If the twentieth century has shown us anything, it has shown us that in the name of our kind of people, we are capable of savagery beyond imagination: Auschwitz, the gulag, the killing fields of Cambodia, the torched villages of Bosnia and Rwanda. We select our friends and we shut everyone else out – by force if necessary.

But we object that this isn't what we're doing in our small group. The fact that I prefer praying with a group of friends to meeting strangers in a church has got nothing to do with ethnic cleansing or racial hatred. James, the Lord's brother, would disagree. In his brief but unsettling letter he links wars and fighting to our greed and exclusiveness (4:1–4), and holds up to us a model of a community where all are welcome regardless of class, race or background, solely on the basis of wanting to follow Jesus.

In a particularly stinging passage, James challenges the small group of Christians meeting around rural Galilee, who were the first recipients of his letter, to welcome all comers equally. 'My brothers and sisters, do you with your acts of favouritism really believe in our glorious Lord Jesus Christ? For if a person with gold rings and in fine clothes comes into your assembly, and if a poor person in dirty clothes also comes in, and if you take notice of the one wearing the fine clothes and say, "Have a seat here, please", while to the one who is poor you say, "Stand there", or "Sit at my feet", have you not made distinctions among yourselves, and become judges with evil thoughts?' (James 2:1–4).

The passage challenges the church (as we saw in the previous chapter) to be open to any and all who are interested in following Jesus – the poor, the homosexual, the alcoholic, the prostitute, the young man with dyed hair and an earring, the middle-aged man in a suit: those who are certainly not our kind of people. We should not duck that challenge.

But equally it is a warning to those of us who want to follow Jesus, but hang back from involvement in the church because it is boring, or full of old folk, or too white, or too black, or too middle-class, or too working-class, or just not attracting people like me. Who am I, to choose whom I'll travel with on the road to the kingdom of God?

The wonder of the church is that it is full of people I wouldn't normally meet, wouldn't have the opportunity to choose as friends, and would never hear speaking about their relationship with Jesus. The wonder is that this is the way God so often speaks to me about my life, my faith, decisions I have to make and problems I have to solve. I have lost count of the number of times a passing remark in a conversation at church has saved me from making a foolish decision or an unwise move, has lifted my spirits when I was feeling down, has given me insight into a passage of Scripture, or has just made me glad to be there that morning. Often the person making that remark has no idea how helpful it has been. Almost invariably that person is someone I wouldn't have met had I not been at church.

It's important to stress, however, that if you're on the edge of a church looking in, it's considerably more difficult to make the first move than if you're on the inside looking out. We're naturally more comfortable with 'people like us'. We're not sure if someone different from us is going accept us and understand where we're coming from. These are genuine concerns. The advantage of the fact that God calls all sorts of people together in his new community in Jesus is that, though I may feel I'm a misfit, I'm actually no more of a misfit than anyone else in this church – including the minister. But the onus must be on the misfits at the centre of things to draw those at the margin into the heart of the church. If they don't, what can we do? We'll come back to that in the last chapter.

Hearing and seeing

It is traditional to think of church as a place where teaching happens. Often, when we think of church, we think of preaching and Bible study. And any good church needs to have both. But, far more importantly, church is a place of learning. And any teacher will tell you that there is a world of difference between teaching and learning.

When I preach a sermon I hope people will learn something. I also hope they'll do something as a result of what they've learned. But if this were the extent of the church's teaching role, we'd be on a hiding to nothing. We need good teaching in church. I believe passionately in the sermon as a teaching vehicle – despite all its detractors (whose arguments are very cogent) and a wealth of educational and communications theory that tells me that sermons can't work. I've seen too many lives changed by preaching, I've been deeply affected too often, myself, to conclude that preaching doesn't have a central place in the life and ministry of the church. But it is not the be-all and end-all of learning. It is only one component, and it is not really the most important one.

The most important component of learning is modelling. If people are to learn, they need to be taught and exhorted, but they also need to be shown. In our society today, all sorts of training schemes include what is called a mentoring element, a period during which we watch someone else doing what we're being taught to do, quiz them on it, and then allow them to watch us as we seek to do what we've been taught. Mentoring programmes are being set up in schools around the country in an attempt to change the behaviour of pupils who seem destined to fail exams and drop out, and who are already getting sidetracked into unhelpful extracurricular activities that are arousing the interest of the police. The aim of such schemes is to link the young person with a young adult who maybe went through similar experiences and temptations, but who has come through to the other side, has landed a good, worthwhile job, and is enjoying life. These young adults become models as well as teachers to the young people; they give them a goal to aim at and a way of hitting the target.

Jesus was a mentor to the first disciples. He didn't just teach them through what he said. He also taught them by what he did. One of the best examples of this is in Luke 11. The disciples have seen Jesus praying, how it affects and drives his ministry, and how it appears to be the key to his ability to do what God wants. So they come to him and ask him to teach them to pray. He gives them the model prayer that we know as the Lord's Prayer. Another example is in Luke 10, when Jesus sends out the seventy disciples to preach and heal. They've been with him and seen the way he operates. Now it's their turn. He gives them instructions (verses 1–16); they go out and put them into practice, and then he debriefs them when they come back. What had they experienced? What had they learned through it? (See verses 17–24.)[5]

Church is a place for mentoring. Not only are we taught the faith, but we also see the faith modelled around us in the lives of people who have been Christians longer than we have, or who have a different life experience from ours. A prime example of this is in the area of marriage. Preachers preach that marriage is the institution created by God for the enjoyment of sex (and the growing emotional intimacy that accompanies healthy sexual union) and for the rearing of children. Increasingly in our society, marriage is no longer the norm. While reports of its death are grossly exaggerated, it is certainly the case that young people are growing up in a world where sex outside of marriage is OK. So it is not enough for the church to teach marriage. It has also got to model it.

Author and teacher Alan Storkey has pointed out that marriage 'is a mature, voluntary union for life based on self-giving and equality before God'. He goes on to lament that 'at present young generations are given few tools to fight for this kind of love against the pressures of the day'.[6]

The world wants to squeeze us into its mould, a mould that says marriage is old-fashioned, that tells us that if love doesn't come naturally we should drop it and move on, and that plays down the Christian virtues of faithfulness and discipline in favour of doing our own thing and seeking our own happiness. These are difficult pressures to resist. One of the tasks of the church is to equip us to resist them and to live the way God wants us to. One way it does this is through teaching and pastoral care. The other, far more crucial way is by modelling Christian marriage in action.

Jack and Molly joined our church. Young and lively, they lived not far away in a tiny flat. They began to make friends and find a place in our family. One day I bumped into Molly, and she said she wanted to speak to me about a delicate issue. We dropped into a cafe and over coffee and Danish pastries she asked me what I thought of marriage. I said I thought it was great. It's what the Bible teaches, but it has also given me twenty-plus very happy years of growing in a relationship with a woman I love more now than when our journey together started. She said she'd been talking to one or two couples in church and observing how they related to each other, and through it she'd reached a decision: she wanted me to marry her and Jack.

I had thought she was about to land me with 'Our marriage is falling apart at the seams', so it was something of a surprise to me that they weren't married – but ministers are often the last people to catch on. I told her I'd be delighted to perform the service. I arranged to meet her and Jack and talk over what was involved, and I got the same story from Jack: how he'd not thought marriage as such was that important – 'Y'know, it's just a piece of paper, that kinda thing' – until he'd started coming to church. He'd met people of all ages at various stages of their married life together. 'But what clinched it was Fred and Dorothy's ruby wedding celebrations,' he said. This couple, members of the church for many years, had requested that we have a special evening service of thanksgiving for their marriage, to which all their church family should be invited. 'I was bowled over by their love and commitment to one another,' Jack recalled. 'I realized that these vows meant something; that it was more than just a piece of paper. I wanted what they had. So I'm asking you to marry us.'

Naturally, I readily agreed, and duly performed the ceremony a few weeks later. There are no guarantees that, forty years down the line, we'll be celebrating Jack and Molly's ruby anniversary at church. But we can be certain that a lot of people will be supporting their marriage by praying for them, talking through issues with them, being there in the tough times, and sometimes even helping them to sort out differences that threaten their relationship.

And what's true of marriage is true of a whole host of lifestyle issues. It is not enough to know what the Bible says. We also need to see biblical principles being modelled around us. Church is where this happens.

We particularly need this when faced by situations where things don't work out. Marriages fall apart – even Christian ones. Leaders fail to live up to the standards they teach. Christians face redundancy, mental breakdown, stress-related illness, trouble with teenage children. How the church responds in these situations is equally vital for modelling Christian teaching.

When a minister I knew had a breakdown and slumped into an awful depression, the church was stunned. It prayed, it felt helpless, it was angry at God for allowing it to happen, but it also stuck by my friend and pulled together to ensure that church kept doing the things it should have been doing. Its response wasn't perfect. The pressure exposed tensions that leaders weren't aware were there. But honesty and humility on their part actually meant that a lot of these tensions proved to be springboards to growth rather than mires that bogged people down in acrimony.

Mike was made redundant in his mid-50s. He took it very badly, believing that at his age he'd never work again, seeing all his plans for early retirement fly out of the window. He felt a failure. He felt he'd let down his family. Several church friends met regularly with him, prayed for him, supported him by looking out for possible job openings, helped out practically when his benefit didn't stretch quite far enough. After several months he landed a job that he wouldn't have got had a church member not spent hours with him teaching him the rudiments of using a computer. Speaking in a church service about the experience he said: 'I felt like the lame man in the gospels, incapable of helping himself, whose friends brought him to Jesus by taking him up on the roof, tearing the tiles away and lowering him down. It wasn't my faith that got me though this – sometimes I'm not sure I had any at all. It was the faith of my friends here in this church.'

At that service, David, who has wondered what practical use church could ever be, was given an answer. 'For the first time, I guess,' he told me over coffee, 'I see that church is for all times but mainly for those times when we really can't make it on our own. I hope I can be one of the guys who brings a friend to Jesus like Mike's mates did. But I also hope others here will do that for me when I need it. From what I've heard, maybe they will.'

It takes all sorts

But more than that is happening in church. I was talking to Peter, a vicar from a northern town who was in London for a conference. We'd not seen each other for years, so we had a lot of catching up to do. He ministers in an urban priority area, very similar to the one I live in. We spoke about success and failure in such ministry. Finally, in the early hours of the morning, I asked him, 'So, what's the gospel for people like this, then?' (I always save the easy questions till last!)

He paused and thought long and hard before he answered: 'It's about feeling good and being together.'

He then told me a story.

His church has a discount store. It is stocked by major retailers who send them end-of-line stuff, last year's high fashion, and returned goods that can't be resold. Members of his congregation love it. They get quality clothes at a price they can afford, and feel good about themselves. But more than that, they are able to sell quality clothes to their neigh-bours, and that makes them feel good, too. 'People feel as though they are helping others as they themselves have been helped. And that makes them feel good,' Peter explained. 'And that couldn't have happened if they hadn't been part of the church. So the church is vital in building people's self-esteem by helping them do things for themselves and others that they couldn't do on their own.'

A frequent reaction to this kind of ministry is the incredu-lous 'I never knew that was the kind of thing the church did!' Sadly, many churches don't do this kind of thing, though they ought to. This is an issue we'll return to in chapters 7 and 8. Equally sadly, some Christians who've given up on the church have done so because they never really stayed long enough to find out what it was all about.

There's a moving scene in Willy Russell's film *Shirley Valentine*. It's the story of stuck-at-home, middle-aged Shirley, who is longing to get away and to get a life. Thinking back to her schooldays, she remembers Marjorie Majors, the girl from the privileged background who had everything Shirley wanted. Now, twenty-five years later, they bump into each other, Shirley out shopping in the rain, Marjorie jumping out of a Rolls-Royce and going to her penthouse apartment. Shirley assumes that her old school friend has acquired her lifestyle as a result of her upbringing and marriage. In fact, Marjorie is a high-class prostitute, returning from one client before jetting off to Paris to join another. Shirley is taken aback. She is even more surprised by the exchange that takes place next. Talking about their schooldays, Marjorie says, 'Did you realize that I wanted to be like you?'

'And I wanted to be like you,' says Shirley. 'If only we'd known, we could have been great mates. Close. You're off to Paris now.'

'But I'd rather be here talking to you,' says Marjorie.

As the two women part, Marjorie embraces and kisses Shirley, who thinks, as she watches the Roller disappear down the road, 'There was real affection in that kiss. The sweetest I'd known for years.'

What a sad encounter!

Our churches, regrettably, are full of Shirleys and Marjories: people who make assumptions about one another, people who judge others by their appearance. And on the basis of the way people look, dress, talk and eat their meals, we make judgments about whether we are going to bother to work at having a relationship with them.

Earlier in the chapter we saw how James urged his readers to give an equal welcome to both one another and the stranger who comes into their meetings. James also urges that we don't judge by appearances. 'You do well', he says, 'if you really fulfil the royal law according to the scripture, "You shall love your neighbour as yourself." But if you show partiality, you commit sin and are convicted by the law as transgressors' (James 2:8–9). Hard, even harsh words. By picking and choosing who in the kingdom of God we'll relate to, we are, says James, breaking the law of God. But we are also robbing ourselves of the opportunity to grow in the faith through forming deep, life-changing relationships with people we are not usually attracted to. We rob ourselves of affection and friendship, as Shirley and Marjorie had done, through judging by appearances.

One of the people whose friendship has been a real help to me in growing as a Christian is Danny. He's Jamaican, and an electrician who's lived in south-east London for years. I'm a grammar-school kid, university educated, and was a journalist. I'd never have met Danny but for the church. Our first meeting was not auspicious. I was being interviewed about the possibility of joining this church as minister. It was going OK until Danny asked me a question. Not being used to his accent, I actually didn't understand a word he said. I thought to myself, 'I'm in trouble here. I can't be minister to people I can't understand.' I muddled through a response. Months later I started work as minister at the church. One of the first people I met as we moved into our new house was Danny. He was doing electrical work in our kitchen, giving up his spare time to make our family home as comfortable as possible.

Over the years, we've talked about life, faith, work, family, the neighbourhood, and the goodness of God. I've learned to understand Danny's way of talking and I've been moved, helped, affirmed, built up, counselled and stimulated by Danny's friendship.

Recently, we moved house. We needed a lot of work doing on our new place, and who should turn up to help with rewiring but Danny. He put in hours to make our new house habitable. On the day we moved, he and his wife Louise looked after our children and cooked us a meal; simple, practical expressions of care and support. Over the meal, Danny expressed his joy that we were staying in the area, and how lovely it was that we would be near neighbours. A few days later they dropped by with a tub of geraniums for the garden.

Maybe it happens elsewhere, but I've never seen it. I wish I could express my appreciation of other people as freely as

Danny can. I hope that through our friendship I will learn to do that. I'd certainly never have enjoyed his friendship or learned so much from it, had I not been in the church.

I'd never have met Eileen either. For thirty years she had struggled with depression. When she came to see me, very early in my ministry, I thought I would counsel her back to health. In fact, she counselled me into reality. Over the few years we knew each other – before her death from cancer – she taught me more about life, especially living with God in the midst of difficulty, than I'd ever learn from books and films. Yet she wasn't my kind of person; she wasn't the kind of woman I would normally meet or get to know. She was God's gift to me through the church, and I am so grateful to him for her.

If we stay in our small corners, if we relate only to those we feel naturally drawn to, we rob ourselves of one of the key ways God uses to help us grow in our faith. That's why the question 'When is it right to leave the church?' is never asked in the New Testament, and is so sad when it's asked today. Church is a gift. It ought to be a place of life and growth, a place where we meet, get to know, learn from, help, support, and are kept going by people we wouldn't normally come across, people God has chosen to put in the melting-pot that is the church.

6 You'll never walk alone

We stood together on the low platform at the front of our church, our arms on one another's shoulders. Cal, Raj and I were praying for one another as a result of something I had said in the sermon that morning. Tomorrow we would be back in our respective workplaces. Church would be a fading memory as deadlines pressed in upon us, relationships with colleagues tested our virtue to the limit, and the boss's expectations more often than not made us feel inadequate and insecure. We prayed, hugged and separated. We'll call each other in the week. But, for the most part, the things we prayed about we'll face alone.

Cal had been telling us that he was facing some really difficult office politics at the moment. People within his organization were jockeying for position and he was feeling squeezed. He felt there was pressure on him to compromise his principles. He said that when he had to face some of these issues with his boss and senior colleagues, he turned to jelly inside, and became a gibbering, inarticulate heap. As we prayed for him, Raj focused on the issue of fear, and I on the fact that under pressure God often gives us the right things to say. But Cal will face the office alone. We can't go with him and hold his hand.

Cal left church that morning stirred and strengthened. The sermon and the time of prayer afterwards had done him good. His confidence was up as he walked out of the building. But tomorrow could be another story as he walks through the door of his office and the recollections and feelings of last week's confrontations flood back in on him. Maybe he'll buckle under the pressure. Perhaps God will answer our prayers, and Cal will overcome his fear and find the words to say in tough meetings. One thing is for sure: by Tuesday, Sunday seems a long way away, the comfort of praying brothers a pleasant but dim memory, the unease of confrontation over the photocopier an all too vivid reality.

With God through the working week?

Church is vital if we are going to live a fruitful and faithful Christian life. But it isn't enough. We also need a daily experience of God, a daily recharging of our batteries. Just how does my experience of God in church on Sunday mesh together with my daily encounter with God in prayer, Bible reading and work through the week? This is a question about spirituality – about how I achieve the integration of my life 'hidden with Christ in God' and my life as seen by my family, my colleagues at work, my team-mates or sports opponents. It is about how I can know the involvement of God in everything I experience, from the sublime peaks of great worship and making love to the depths of conflict at work or home, and through to the ordinary jogging along of my daily routines. And it's about the role church plays in that.

I once worked in the same organization as a guy who was a youth leader in a large evangelical church. At weekends he ran Bible classes, and during the week he was an advertising sales executive. His two worlds were separated by a long train ride into London from the sticks, and during that long train ride, he underwent a spiritual metamorphosis. On the way into town he became, to dispassionate observers who knew nothing of his weekend life, just another hard-drinking, foul-mouthed businessman who went for the jugular, pursued the deal, ripped off his clients and shafted his colleagues if it was to his advantage. He sold a lot of advertising and thus endeared himself to the people upstairs. On the way home he reverted to being a Bible-believing, clean-living person who played a part in his church's care for its young people.

This man was an extreme example of something that is not unusual. The workplace is tough on Christians. It is much easier to blend in with the crowd, and that means joining in the office politics, the cutting remarks about colleagues, and the bad-mouthing of management. It often means that to be accepted you need to tell good jokes (usually dirty ones) and stand your round in the pub (and be able to stand up when everyone else has stood theirs!). This young ad sales executive was just trying to survive. It wasn't that church didn't mean much to him – his commitment to its youth work showed that it did. It wasn't that he had no faith – I'm sure he really believed. And it wasn't that he didn't see a problem – he did. In about the only candid conversation I had with him, he recognized that sometimes he went over the top at work, and that he failed to live, as he put it, 'by the regulations'. I believe his survival tactics were wrong, and that if he had found a way of integrating what he was doing, learning and praying on Sunday with what he was involved in during the week, he would have found a better way to survive – a way that didn't leave him, in his more honest moments (often late at night when he was alone), feeling wracked with guilt at his failure to live up to his faith.

Someone meeting him at work and hearing that he was a Christian would probably have been surprised. If pressed, they'd probably have called him a hypocrite, someone who conceals his true character or belief when away from his church. For those outside the church, it would confirm a popular stereotype of Christians: that we are all hypocrites, whose faith, given its total lack of effect on our lifestyle, cannot amount to very much.

Jesus spoke a lot about hypocrisy, and looking at what he said in the context within which he said it helps us to understand just what hypocrisy is and isn't. Much more importantly, it helps us to get a handle on the nature of true spirituality, and the relationship between our outer life at church and at work and our inner life of prayer and growth in our Christian faith.

But before launching into what Jesus says, let's pause and think about what our young ad man could do to live a more consistent life. I think there are a number of things he could build into his weekday life to help him to integrate what happens in church with what happens at work. And they're things all of us could do as well.

The first is to get a small group of people at church praying regularly for him. Paul worked in a drug rehabilitation project in Pakistan. He told me that in order to maintain consistency at work, he prayed every week with a couple of other guys. At the start they were not close friends, but over time they grew to be, because every week they confessed their sins to one another (see James 5:16) and they confessed their areas of struggle – what the situations were that most tempted them. Within the small group, they held one another accountable. Sometimes it was painful, usually it was difficult (and very easy to find an excuse for missing the meeting), but always it brought Paul closer to God and strengthened him for whatever the week threw at him. Our young ad man would have benefited from such a group. Would you?

The second is to try to meet Christians in or around work sometime during the week. Maybe people in the same business who face the same pressures. Some larger companies have Christian unions, and many town-centre and city-centre churches have mid-week services designed to fit a lunch break. We need to seek these things out. We need to make time to go to them. If we do, we'll find our faith given the boost it needs in the midst of the working week.

The third is to take Jesus at his word and recognize that the Christian faith is not about keeping the rules or even keeping up appearances. It's about having a relationship with Jesus, based on trust, knowing that he accepts us whatever we've done, is prepared to forgive us and help us to move on, and is always willing to give us his Holy Spirit, just at the time we need it, when temptation is at its most acute. Let's explore this further.

Religion, rules and relationship

Jesus didn't seem to hit it off with religious people. It doesn't take long, reading the Gospels, to come across incidents where he is at loggerheads with the most religious people of his day, the Pharisees. It is all too easy for us to dismiss the Pharisees as a bunch of holier-than-thou, legalistic no-hopers. The truth is that, as we saw earlier, they were the charismatic evangelicals of the first century. They believed in the Holy Spirit and the authority of Scripture, unlike most other groups in first-century Judaism. Indeed, it was their belief in the authority of Scripture that made them so zealous for rules. For instance, the Scripture said that the people should keep the sabbath day holy and not do any work on it. The Pharisees asked themselves, 'How do we apply this word to our everyday lives?' They lived mainly in agricultural communities. Life couldn't stop just because it was Saturday and God had said to keep it special for him. So they made a set of rules that laid down what they could and couldn't do on the sabbath. This was part of their spirituality, a way of taking their faith so seriously that it affected every area of their lives.

Then along came Jesus, who seemed to flout all these rules. He didn't keep their sabbath regulations; he played fast and loose with food laws; he mixed with unsavoury people. The Pharisees attacked him for it. And you can understand why. He seemed to be undermining everything they held dear; but, worse than that, he threatened to undermine the entire system of spirituality the Pharisees had built up and taught their people to follow. If he succeeded, what would become of the people's faith?

Luke records two incidents involving things Jesus did on the sabbath that caused offence (see Luke 6). First, he allowed his disciples to work. They were in a cornfield, running their hands along the heads of grain, picking off the husk and eating the ripe grain inside. This was classified as harvesting and threshing – both activities strictly banned on the sabbath as non-essential work. Then Jesus went into a synagogue and found a man with a withered hand, called him over and healed him in full view of everyone. He didn't have to do it then. The man's hand had been withered for ever. It would be withered tomorrow. Jesus could have healed him then in the privacy of his own home. But Jesus chose to heal him on the sabbath. And it seemed as though he did it publicly to offend the Pharisees.

Just before these events, he'd been upsetting the Pharisees over whom he ate with. He had singled out Levi, a tax collector, and said, 'Follow me' (Luke 5:27). Levi had thrown a banquet for Jesus and his friends that was attended by all sorts of local low life. Tax collectors were the Mafia of first-century Palestine. They were not the kind of people religious folk mixed with. But Jesus did. Then he got into a dispute over fasting. The Pharisees, their disciples, John the Baptist and his disciples all fasted. But Jesus and his disciples didn't. Indeed, Jesus was getting a bit of a reputation for being a party animal, always eating and drinking with dodgy company.

The religious folk didn't like it. He seemed to them to be a hypocrite. He went to the synagogue on the sabbath, where he heard the law read and worshipped the Lord. During the week, he ate with people who were ritually unclean, he didn't fast as a way of showing his loyalty to God and – horror of horrors – he didn't really keep the sabbath because he healed on it and allowed his disciples to work. Jesus, for his part, called the Pharisees hypocrites and saved some of his harshest words for them. What was going on?

It all had to do with who Jesus was and why he came. In Luke 6 it is clear that Jesus' reason for doing what he did on the sabbath was to demonstrate to the people who saw him that he was something special and that they'd better pay attention to what he said. 'The Son of Man is lord of the sabbath,' he told them (verse 5). 'Son of Man' is Jesus' favourite title (appearing here, significantly, for the first time in Luke's Gospel). It is derived from Daniel 7:13, where the prophet had seen a vision of one like a son of man ascending to heaven and being given all authority over earth and heaven. By the first century there is some evidence that the term had become a title associated with the expected Messiah. Jesus used it because it had an air of mystery about it. But there was no mystery about what he was claiming when he said, 'The Son of Man is lord of the sabbath.' He was clearly claiming an authority equal to that of Moses (who had given the people of Israel the law regarding the sabbath) and even of God (who had told Moses what to say).

But it wasn't just what Jesus was claiming for himself that was upsetting the religious folk of his day – though it was enough to give most of them a seizure. It was also the nature of his mission. In the calling of Levi and other similarly unsuitable people to be his friends and associates, he was giving a clear signal that everyone was welcome in his community – which he called the kingdom of God – regardless of their lifestyle and of how well they had observed the rules. He said, in effect, that belonging preceded believing, something we looked at in some detail in chapter 4.

He also said that life in his community was less like going to church and more like being at a party. When asked about fasting, he told his inquisitors that you don't fast when the bridegroom is around. He was saying that life in his merry band was like a never-ending wedding feast. The reason the disciples at the beginning of Luke 6 were so relaxed about plucking and eating grain on the sabbath was that they had tasted the new wine of being in Jesus' band of followers. They had experienced a new freedom that allowed them to stop looking over their shoulders, concerned all the time about what other people thought, especially the religious leaders. They knew (because Jesus had told them this) that God accepted them as they were, not because they kept the law, but because he loved them.

Of course, Jesus was really only reminding people of what had been true when the sabbath was instituted. Back when Moses gave the law that contained the commandment to take Saturdays off, the people of Israel had already been rescued from Egypt. Sabbath came after salvation; law came after liberty. Indeed, in Deuteronomy 5:12–15 the people are reminded that one reason they were to observe the sabbath was that it gave them opportunity to pause and remember their rescue from slavery in Egypt. Sabbath was meant to celebrate freedom, not restrict it by making people feel guilty.

What this all amounts to is that Jesus calls people to a spirituality of relationship, not of rules; of friendship with God, not of formulas and codes of law; a spirituality that is based on the wonderful fact of God's love for each one of us, regardless of how we've lived, what we've said or done, or who we are. Jesus invited Levi to come and join him on his journey. He didn't interview him to suss out his beliefs on the authority of the Scriptures and on whether the rapture will happen before, during or after the tribulation. He invited the man with the withered hand to come and experience healing. He didn't first examine his faith or ask him whether he had prayed about this in the past. Jesus invites people into relationship with him because he wants everyone to get to know him, regardless of their track record or past misdeeds.

Religious people struggle with this, because religion is about rules. It's about finding a formula, a code of practice to live by. When faced by decisions, religious people consult the rule-book to see what's allowed, what's forbidden, what's set down on tablets of stone. Jesus says, 'Come with me. Let's chill a while, get to know each other, travel the road together.' Religious people can't cope with this, so they have to get rid of him (Luke 6:11).

Kingdom spirituality

Jesus creates a new community of God's people based on his invitation to come and join him on his journey. He gives it formal shape by calling twelve of his first followers to be a special inner circle (Luke 6:12–16). Jesus is here self-consciously refounding Israel, which was established from the twelve sons of Jacob. And then he gives shape to what this new spirituality is like, and how the people who belong to this community of Jesus people will behave towards each other and live in the world (Luke 6:17–49). By healing and by allowing his disciples to harvest on a Saturday, Jesus was saying that on his sabbath there would be healing and feeding of hungry people, because this was what his kingdom, his spirituality, was about. By talking of sharing our lives with the poor, loving our enemies and not being judgmental towards one another, he is spelling out the kind of attitudes people in his community should exhibit.

Luke 6 is not the only place where Jesus details the spirituality of the kingdom of God. In the Sermon on the Mount in Matthew 5 – 7, Jesus also talks about the lifestyle of his friends. He gives us lessons on prayer, giving and fasting (yes, it does have a place), and he especially focuses on the core values that motivate us. 'What are you living for?' he asks. 'You cannot serve God and money,' he says. The spirituality of the kingdom is rooted in dependence on God, but not removed from the normal daily round. The key is where our treasure is, says Jesus: are we working for money or to serve God? Are we giving to look good, or out of gratitude for all that God has done for us? Are we fasting so that people will marvel at our holiness, or so that we can spend time praying when we would usually be eating, our mild hunger pangs reminding us of our dependence on God for all things?

This is a spirituality that is taken up by the New Testament's first theologians, the people who struggled to grasp the significance of what God was up to in Jesus for everyday life beyond the resurrection. Paul, for instance, has much to say about our attitudes towards one another within the household of faith and towards those in the world who do not share our way of life. He doesn't have much time for religion, however. As we have already seen, in Galatians he spells out what it means for Jew and Gentile to be one in Christ: an end to the works of the law; that is the religious practices – circumcision, dietary regulations, keeping the sabbath – that separated Jew from Gentile. It seems unlikely that Paul would have joined the Keep Sunday Special campaign on religious grounds! Rather, our inclusion within the people of God is based on faith in Jesus alone. So we should accept one another regardless of ethnic background or religious preferences, because Jesus makes us one with one another.

More than that, religious observance has become redundant because of the coming of the Spirit. Through the sacrifice of Jesus, we are set free from our sins (and from religion) and filled with the Spirit of Jesus. Therefore, says Paul, we should live as the Spirit directs us to. Instead of being ruled by our glands, following the whim of our flesh, taking the easy way out, and living solely to please ourselves, we should be led by the Spirit, he says (see Galatians 5:13 – 6:10). This is partly effort on our part, and partly the work of God, who grows in us the lovely fruit of the Spirit, the qualities that marked Jesus' life. Christian spirituality is about a partnership between the believer and Jesus.

In many ways, as we've already seen, it is summed up in Romans 12:1–2, where Paul says that in view of the mercies of God we should 'present [our] bodies as a living sacrifice, holy and acceptable to God, which is [our] spiritual worship'. We should 'not be conformed to this world, but be transformed by the renewing of [our] minds, so that [we] may discern what is the will of God – what is good and acceptable and perfect'. For Paul, spirituality is seen in the way we live our lives in the world, not in pious talk at the church prayer meeting. For him, what shows our relationship with God is the way we do our work, conduct ourselves at home, and regard other people, not whether we can preach a great sermon or sing in tongues.

Get your head round this!

This is why Paul was so concerned about our minds and our thinking. Christian spirituality is as much about the mind as it is about wonderful experiences of union with God. Yes, it is important that we have great experiences. No-one wants a dry, arid Christianity that is all concept and no feeling, all sound doctrine with every 't' crossed and every 'i' dotted. We are creatures who need to feel the rush of ecstasy in prayer and worship, and the outpouring of emotion when we feel the touch of God, whether that be in tears or laughter or dancing, or a warm glow inside that makes us feel good despite the rain, the pressure at work and our money worries.

But Christian spirituality is also about thinking great thoughts, God's thoughts. It is about setting our minds on the truth, thinking it through, grappling with it intensely, and wrestling with it until it makes sense (or enough sense for us to live with it). In Ephesians 4, having explained what the church is for and how every member has a role in building it up, Paul says, 'Now this I affirm and insist on in the Lord: you must no longer live as the Gentiles live, in the futility of their *minds*. They are darkened in their *understanding*, alienated from the life of God because of their *ignorance* and *hardness of heart* … That is not the way you *learned* Christ! For surely you have *heard* about him and were *taught* in him, as *truth* is in Jesus. You were *taught* to put away your former way of life, your old self, corrupt and deluded by its lusts, and to be renewed in the spirit of your *minds*' (verses 17–23). Notice the number of words, which I've put in italics, that have to do with thinking and the mind.

Too often Christian spirituality is perceived as being only about how we feel, about the experiences we have. Too often we are told that all we need is an experience that elevates us to a new plane of living – an encounter with God that washes all our old attitudes away and replaces them with lovely new ones. Worse, sometimes we are told that all we need is to be delivered of a 'spirit' of our old attitudes or way of life, and then everything will be OK.

Helen came to see me once. She was clearly unhappy. She had been for a while. She's a middle-aged lady brought up in a strict Christian home, schooled in the traditional evangelical disciplines of a daily quiet time and weekly attendance at church on Sunday and the Bible study during the week. But recently, it just wasn't cutting it any more. She felt inadequate and hopeless as a Christian. And on this morning, she came looking for something that would put it right. 'I feel such a failure,' she said. 'I'm not making any progress at all in my Christian life. I feel I need something, a zap of the Spirit, something to make me change.'

She asked me to pray for her. I suggested we talk first. I was keen to know where her dissatisfaction came from. You see, there is a genuine restlessness that is stirred in our spirit by the Spirit of God, spurring us on to growth in our Christian lives. But there is also a dissatisfaction born of the preaching of the quick-fix merchants, those who say that a particular experi-ence is all we need to jump-start our spiritual lives and help us to enter into a new dimension of powerful, effective Christian living. If only! I learned that she'd been at a meeting over the past weekend where just such a religious product was on offer. It had made her unhappy with her life as it was, but it hadn't offered her a solution that worked. She'd been prayed for, but felt no different. And she blamed herself.

I turned with her to Ephesians 4 and Colossians 3, and we discovered together that the Christian life is not about great experiences giving us a leg-up to new planes of living. It is about making decisions to change our thinking and behaviour, and about the way that, as we do so, God works in us to grow the wonderful fruit of a life like Jesus Christ's. It is great to be prayed for. It is wonderful when God touches our life in a special way at a meeting and we come away glowing inside. We can never have enough encounters of this kind. But we cannot build a life on these experiences alone. We also need the regular daily and weekly discipline of bringing our thinking and attitudes into line with those of our Lord.

In Colossians 3, after telling us that our true life is hid with Christ in God, and that we should set our minds (that word again!) on things that are above, Paul tells us to strip off certain attitudes and ways of behaving and then put on others. It is something we do, like taking off one set of rather grubby clothes and putting on freshly laundered and ironed ones. Paul does not tell us to 'get delivered' from these things. He says we are responsible for changing our behaviour, albeit with the help of God. 'Put to death, therefore, whatever in you is earthly,' he says (verse 5). 'Do not lie to one another, seeing that you have stripped off the old self with its practices' (verse 9). We must 'get rid of ' the kind of behaviour that belongs to the life of disobedience (verse 8). These are commands, instructions that require us to do something. The implication is that no-one else – not even God – can or will do it for us.

Then, in verses 12–14, he tells us to put on certain things – compassion, kindness, humility, meekness, patience, love – qualities that are seen perfectly in Jesus. These are aspects of

God's character, and because we are made in his image they ought to be aspects of our characters. But sin has warped and distorted them in us. Salvation is about being remade in the image of God.

And how does this happen? It starts in the mind. Our new self, says Paul, is being renewed in knowledge according to the image of its creator (verse 10). And the knowledge comes from the word of Christ, he explains in verse 16: 'Let the word of Christ dwell in you richly; teach and admonish one another in all wisdom.' Our minds are transformed by encountering the word of Christ, or, as Paul puts it in Ephesians, the truth.

Remember the advertising sales executive we met earlier in the chapter? What was happening in his mind? How was he feeding his thinking through the week? Often we struggle because we starve ourselves of the nourishment our minds need to keep our relationship with God vibrant and alive.

Encountering the Word

This is why the Bible has a central place in Christian spirituality. We need to read it, grapple with it, argue with it, rage at it, sit under it, hang on to it, and let it seep into our thinking so that it shapes our attitudes and actions. Paul, of course, did not have in mind five minutes at the start of the day with our pocket Bible and daily-reading aid. For a start, most of his congregations didn't have Bibles. Furthermore, most of the first hearers of his letters couldn't have read one even if they did. For those early Christians, the words of Scripture were passed on orally, learned in great chunks and chewed over as they went about their daily routines.

We live in a culture that, sadly, has very little memory. There is a story from the ancient Near East about the invention of writing. In it the gods warn people that writing will lead to forgetting. How true that is! In our generation, we have access to more information through libraries, computers and the internet than any generation in history. Yet we are also very forgetful. Because the information is at our fingertips, we don't bother to learn it. After all, we tell ourselves, we know where to look it up. This is fine for most things. But it is not helpful for our spirituality. Paul doesn't say, 'Let the word of Christ dwell richly in a book or on a computer disk or on a website.' He says, 'Let the word of Christ dwell in *you* richly.'

How will this happen? The classic evangelical answer is that it happens through a daily quiet time and a weekly injection of teaching in the form of a sermon. And sadly, that still seems to be the best mixture. I say 'sadly' because I wish I had something new and improved to offer, a super-fast track to the knowledge that will transform our minds and inspire us to live godly lives. Unfortunately no such fast track exists. And I do not want to join the ranks of the quick-fix merchants who offer what doesn't exist.

The daily quiet time has fallen into disrepute, partly because of the legalistic way it has been taught in the past, and partly because we are ill-disciplined. But there are creative ways of ensuring that we imbibe the Word of God that are worth exploring, because they will inject life and vitality into a process which for many – me included – can be little more than a dutiful slog.

My friend Steve gets the bus to work in central London. He gets off on the south side of the river Thames and walks across the bridge to his office on the other side. As he walks, he prays. He talks to God about everything that happened at work yesterday and that is going to happen today. He describes how helpful it is to walk and pray, the rhythm of his movement helping him to concentrate on what he is saying to God. One of the things he does during this time is to mull over what he heard in church on Sunday and how it might apply in the office today. The grand word for this is 'meditation'.

Meditation is a bit like sucking a boiled sweet. We roll it around our mouths, exploring its surface with our tongue, sensing how it changes shape as it slowly dissolves. It is something we do with relish and delight. In Isaiah 31:4 the prophet says, 'As a lion or a young lion growls over its prey ...' The Hebrew word he uses for 'growls over' is the one the Psalms use when they talk about meditating on the law of the Lord. The idea is that a lion takes time with its kill, purrs over it, savours it, and ensures that it gets every bit of nourishment out of it that it can. After all, it could be a while before another hapless wildebeest crosses its path.

Meditation is the slow way of reading Scripture. It is very valid and helpful but takes a lot of patience. We are such restless people, tracking down the info, absorbing it and moving on. Meditation says, 'Slow down, pause a while, graze, take your time.' It is so easy to miss things if we rush. The trouble is that our culture doesn't encourage us to slow down, and church culture apes the world in this. I'm sure we've all had conversations with people who've come back from Christian conferences with what they describe as 'spiritual indigestion'. They've been bombarded with so much information that they have lost their capacity to process any of it. This isn't surprising. Just imagine that all the information imparted by the average Christian Bible week was a meal. By the time we'd eaten a tenth of it, we'd be feeling pretty stuffed and would need to take a break to allow our digestion time to work before getting stuck into more. Dieticians tell us that eating little and often is better for our overall health than consuming plates heaving with food at one sitting. I'm sure the same is true of ingesting the Word of God.

Sometimes I read something in the Bible that stops me dead in my tracks. It might be something I've never noticed before. It might be something I'm very familiar with but which hits me with a fresh force. The worst thing I can do at this point is to say, 'Oh, that's interesting', and then move on. What I have to do is stop and think about it. What is this passage, phrase or sentence saying? Not just 'What is it saying to me?' but what is it saying about God, the world, the church, work, home, family or culture? I need to mull the words over, treat them as I would a boiled sweet, take my time over them, ponder them, and wonder how they apply to the world as I see it, and what difference they'll make to my perceptions of God and his kingdom and to my role within it. Sometimes this process of sucking on a word can take a week or more. I come back to read it again and again. I look it up in different versions. I'll even read it in the original language and then rush to the commentaries to tell me what the words mean and how they were used in various contexts. I milk it for every nuance of meaning there is to find in it before I move on.

Now this doesn't happen every day or even every month. Possibly half a dozen times a year. But those times are rich in growth and development. At other times I am reading large chunks of the Bible at one sitting, or not reading the Bible at all because I am listening to music or reading something else that is making me think about God, his world and my place in it. I find that God speaks to me through all sorts of music. Recently I've been set thinking and praying by artists as diverse as U2, Joan Osborne, Eels, Blur, The Verve, Lowgold, Nick Drake and Bruce Cockburn.

A couple of years ago I was leading a youth weekend. As part of the programme there was a compulsory time of quiet each day where we were all expected to read or listen to our Walkmans. I did both. I was listening to Radiohead's *The Bends* while reading 2 Timothy in Euguene Peterson's excellent paraphrase of the New Testament, *The Message*. I'd decided to read the whole letter at one sitting without pausing to mine the meaning of individual words or phrases. I'd reached the place where Paul is telling Timothy that 'Every part of Scripture is God-breathed and useful in one way or another ...' (2 Timothy 3:16). I've got to admit that at this point I was probably paying more attention to the music than to the Bible, and I was finding it hard to keep my eyes open. Late nights were catching up with me.

But the next sentence snapped me awake. I sat bolt upright and paid close attention. As Radiohead's Thom Yorke spat 'Everything is broken' over a wash of fuzzed and jagged guitars, I read: 'Through the Word we are put together and shaped up for the tasks God has for us' (verse 17). Wow! Yorke's analysis of the world – such as it is – is spot on. Everything is broken; I'm broken. But the wonder of the good news is that God puts us back together again and does so through his Word. Not only that; through the Bible he shapes us for the tasks he wants us to do – one of which is taking to people like Thom Yorke the message of how God mends the broken.

My senses were working overtime. I felt alert and excited about what God was saying. I don't think I would have heard it had I just been reading the Bible or just been listening to Radiohead. It was doing both at once that set me up to hear God's message for me that day.[1]

Of course, none of this has a direct bearing on my relationship with church. I can meditate on Scripture, read my Bible and pray-walk my way to work whether I'm involved in a church or not. But I believe that church affects our personal spiritual lives in two absolutely crucial ways. The first is that it can set the agenda for the way we think about God and respond to him this week.

Thought for the week

In the last chapter I told you about how Alex had had us all putting together a jigsaw of God's characteristics one Sunday morning. She'd asked us what colour we thought of when we thought about God, what place God had been special to us in, and so on. Well, that relatively short slot in the service gave me much to think about and process through the week.

At various times in the succeeding days I had often found myself pondering the places where I had been acutely aware of God. The place that most readily comes to mind at the moment is Hope Cove in Devon. It was where I had walked and shouted at God the day Ellie died. It was where I became aware of his presence in that moment of acute darkness. In the week after Alex had led the service, I thought about that day quite a lot. It is a memory that still smarts with pain. When I dwell on it, I am caught up afresh in all the emotions and unanswered questions of that time. I wrestle again with the problem of unanswered prayer and undeserved suffering – big questions that never get answered but which we learn to live with as we talk them over with God.

But other thoughts come to mind as well as the painful memories. I remember to pray for John and his son – Ellie's son – Cameron. I remember to pray for others in our church who were particularly affected by Ellie's death and who still bear the scars. I remember to give thanks for the support the church was to so many as we travelled together through the dark valley. In the week following the service Alex led, I was much taken with these thoughts. I would not have been, had she not led us the way she did. In many ways, she suggested the direction for my prayer life over the few days after that service.

Other things happen in church that are equally agenda-setting. We hear sermons that often provoke us to think about the subject or the passage of Scripture being preached on. Many's the time I've made a short note to myself to follow something up as a result of what was said. And often that study and meditation have led me to a fresh encounter with God, not in the service but during the week after it. I know this happens to other people as well, because they've come to talk to me about it – an occupational hazard of being a preacher that I'm only too happy to be on the receiving end of.

Max was riled by something I said in a sermon. The trouble was, it was really a throwaway line, an aside that hadn't been in my notes but had seemed the right thing to say at the time. Max thought it wasn't. I'd been talking about forgiveness: about how, because God forgives us, we ought to forgive one another. The throwaway line that so upset Max was about God's forgiveness of us being dependent on our forgiving other people. I didn't develop it; perhaps I should have done, but I'd already been speaking for too long.

Max said that he'd heard other preachers saying it but never justifying it, and that he found it difficult to take. After all, God's grace was freely given in Jesus, he said; as far as the east is from the west, that's how far God puts our sins from us. I agreed, and apologized for not elaborating on my remark. I suggested that he read Matthew 6:14–15 (where Jesus talks about forgiveness); ponder the line in the Lord's Prayer, 'Forgive us our debts, as we also have forgiven our debtors ...' (verse 12) and read the parable of the unmerciful slave (Mathew 18:23–35). We were at a conference, and lots of people wanted to talk to me, so Max and I didn't have long to chat. I didn't see him the next day, or the next – he didn't come to the evening meetings, and I didn't see him at any of the daytime sports activities or walks. Finally, he came and sat next to me at breakfast on the third day.

'Yeah. I've been thinking about what you said. I read the passages you told me to, and thought about how forgiveness is part of God's character and so ought to be part of ours as Christians,' he said. 'I guess if we can't or won't forgive, we haven't got the hang of it, and so God can't really forgive us either. Thanks.'

I had given direction to his spiritual life over the past few days as he wrestled with whether my aside had been right or wrong. I hope it had helped him to grow in his understanding of his faith and knowledge of his God.

It isn't just the preaching or worship at church that can set the agenda for our spiritual lives over the coming week. It is also the conversation. Paul said we should let the word of Christ dwell in us richly. He also said that we should speak the truth in love – by which he did not mean that we tell someone they're inadequate with a smile on our face! Rather, 'truth' here refers to the message about Jesus and his kingdom, and we should tell it to one another to build one another up because we love one another and long to see one another grow in our faith.

When the service ends at our church, the talking starts. Over tea and coffee, for at least the next hour, people chat about all kinds of things. Some of it is business – people on various committees touching base, the treasurer checking out Gift Aid forms … you know the sort of thing. A lot of it is good gossip: 'What kind of week have you had?' 'How's work?' 'Family OK?' Some of it is passing on the truth in love. It is brother and sister helping each other with a problem, talking over an issue at work – much as Cal, Raj and I were doing at the beginning of this chapter. Sometimes it ends in praying. Often it sets the course for our praying and reading of Scripture during the week.

This is good, healthy church life. We need to encourage it. But we also need to be aware of those on the edges. Are we helping them to join in the conversation? And, once invited, are those on the margins joining in? It is often those who are not at the centre of things who bring the most interesting perspectives on issues of life and faith.

Eileen and Peggy were talking one Sunday over coffee. Peggy's husband, George, is not a Christian. Eileen came to faith late in life, so she can remember what it is like to get a hard time for going to church. Peggy had had a particularly tough week with George, and was at her wits' end. Eileen encouraged her, not only by sharing how the Scriptures had helped her when she was in that situation, but also by suggesting passages Peggy could read over the coming days.

Diane hung around on the edge of our church for months. Her kids came to Sunday school because, frankly, it got them out from under her feet for an hour or so on a Sunday. She herself came occasionally. But though she wanted to belong, she didn't think church was for people like her …

So we invited her to host a 'just looking' group. This killed two birds with one stone. It gave us a neutral, non-church venue for our group to meet in. But more importantly, it told Diane that she belonged. We read Luke's Gospel in her flat every other week for the best part of a year. She loved it. She loved hosting the group – making us tea and coffee, remembering what everyone liked, choosing different biscuits every time we came round – and she loved joining in. For the first time in her life, people listened to what she thought about things. And for the first time in her life, she realized that God cared about her and that she had a place within his people. She came on Sunday to find out what was going to happen at the group in her house and to talk to others about how it was good to host it. She came even when her children didn't, because she had grown to feel a part of what was happening on Sunday as well as midweek.

Staying on message

There is a second way in which church affects our personal spiritual lives. Involvement with others can save us from becoming eccentric in our spirituality. Now we have to be careful here. There are as many ways of being a Christian as there are people in the world. Each of us is unique, and the last thing we want is to be squeezed into someone's mould, especially a mould made by a church leader in a nylon shirt. There is plenty of room for variety and diversity. Indeed, one of the wonderful things about the church is the rich mixture of experiences and insights gathered under one roof on the average Sunday.

But because we are unique and because we are fallen, there is always a danger that we will express our spirituality in an idiosyncratic way. We may think thoughts or have ideas and hunches that, frankly, are a little odd. Left to ourselves, these ideas get built up into whole doctrinal systems. The evidence of this is plain for all to see in the various cults and weird fringe groups that have grown up around leaders whose insights into the spiritual life seem to owe more to strong Cheddar eaten late at night than to the inspiration of the Holy Spirit. Church helps us to keep our eccentricities in check.

Gerald felt that God was calling him to preach. This was not unexpected, though, having talked with him over the past few months, I did think it was unlikely. I thought the best way to help Gerald to test out his call was to set him the task of preparing a sermon on a particular passage of Scripture. We settled on Matthew 5:1–12 and fixed a meeting for two weeks' time. I cannot begin to describe the sermon outline that confronted me a fortnight later. The reading of the text was so off-beam that I really did not know where to begin in critiquing the sermon. So I asked him what commentaries and reference books he had used. He replied that he hadn't; he had 'just relied on the Spirit to guide him'. Sadly, Gerald is not alone. There are lots of people like him out there – some of them rather more prominent in leadership, especially on the conference circuit, than seems good for the long-term health of the church.

We chatted about why it's helpful to use commentaries and reference works when trying to understand what a passage of Scripture is saying. This is why sermons are so crucial to the teaching ministry of the church. In a sermon we unpack the meaning of a particular text, or expound a particular doctrine or a Christian view on a topical issue. Good sermons are the result of a lot of interaction between the preacher and the world of scholarship, through the use of commentaries and reference works. Even better sermons are the result of that interaction plus good knowledge of, and interaction with, the congregation being preached to. This is one reason why conference ministry is potentially dangerous; the preacher is rarely accountable to the congregation, certainly not anything like as accountable as a local church minister is.

But church doesn't just keep ministers in check. It helps all of us to watch over one another in love, as Ron Sider put it in *Rich Christians in an Age of Hunger*.[2] One of the reasons for speaking the truth to each other in love is that we are concerned that each member of our church should grow into a healthy, mature Christian. As we get to know one another through regular interaction at church, so we are able to sound one another out on what the passages we've read mean, or how we handle certain situations that have arisen in our lives.

The great thing about the Christian life is that we don't have to make it up as we go along. Others have lived it before us. Others are living it now around us. There is a wealth of experience and wisdom that we can tap into right now on our doorstep. When we join the Christian journey, although we have to work out our own salvation with fear and trembling (as Paul says in Philippians 2:12), we don't have to do it alone. That passage is yet another one bristling with plural pronouns and verbs of the kind we were thinking about in the previous chapter. We work it out in fellowship with others. Christian spirituality is, almost by definition, a corporate spirituality.

Of course, we all have our own relationship with Jesus; we all travel our own path to maturity guided by the Holy Spirit. As Paul goes on to say in Philippians 2:13, 'God ... is at work in you, enabling you both to will and to work for his good pleasure.' One of the ways God helps us to reach maturity is through one another. The 'you' in Philippians 2:13 is again a plural 'you', and the verse could be translated to say that God is at work 'among you' to help you all together to want the things of God and to achieve them in your lives. The implication is that we are helping one another to achieve this. For these words come at the end of a section that begins with an appeal to unity (2:1–4) based on imitating Jesus (2:5–11), the model of our spirituality.

We need one another. 'As iron sharpens iron, so one man sharpens another' (Proverbs 27:17, New International

Version). Our spiritual lives get blunt, lose their cutting edge and become useless if we lose this corporate dimension.

How can we help to make all this much more of a reality in the churches to which we belong? That's the topic of our final chapter. But first we need to look at how churches in the twenty-first century, and not just individual Christians, are struggling to find their place in a rapidly changing culture.

7 Will rearranging the deckchairs be sufficient?

The church, as we saw in the Introduction, is getting deeper and deeper into trouble. And those troubles make life harder for those who already struggle with it. The question is: can a struggling church and those who wonder if they'll ever find a place within it actually come to each other's aid and, through a constructive conversation, create communities that better reflect the New Testament's picture of church, the picture we tried to paint in chapters 2–4? That's the theme of the next chapter. In this one, we'll plumb the depth of the hole in which the church finds itself.

The church, as one cultural vessel among many, finds itself in troubled waters. On the one hand, the ship of the church is itself foundering in the cross-currents of cultural transition. And on the other, it has become a sort of hospital ship, attracting refugees from a former era who find in it hope of return to more familiar waters. To employ a much-overworked analogy, there is a good deal of rearranging of the deckchairs, not to mention angry arguments on the bridge. Meanwhile some distressed passengers are leaping overboard, preferring their chances in the open sea.[1]

This is a great image of the troubles the church faces. It points to the confusion among leaders as well as the concern many members feel. Recently I was at a party and the conversation turned to church. Most of the guests loitering around the food table attended the same one. Professional, gifted and committed, they each expressed concern that there appeared to be a growing gulf between them and their fellowship; in short, it seemed the church had lost touch with their lives.

'I don't hear anything on Sunday that helps me during the week,' said Mike.

Griff added that the leaders didn't seem to listen any more. 'The minister has his programme and seems to see it as his mission to get that programme up and running regardless of what any of us think.'

Penny chimed in with, 'I want to be involved and support what's going on. I hate being critical, but I resent not being taken seriously as someone with gifts and something to offer, not just to the doing, but also to the thinking and planning.'

I know their minister and his story is, not surprisingly, somewhat different. 'The church is drifting and needs to get back a sense of purpose,' he told me over a pint. 'The trouble is that everyone wants it to grow and attract new people, but at the same time they want it to meet their needs. And no-one seems able to give more than a Sunday morning and a home-group evening to it because they're so busy. What am I supposed to do?'

This church is not untypical. Up and down the land people struggle to make a connection between what happens in church on Sunday and their working lives, while ministers juggle increasing demands for Sunday-school and youth provision, coffee after the service, smaller home groups and more outreach to the community, with the fact that fewer and fewer people seem to be willing to take on leadership roles in any of these areas of the church's life. The minister of a 500-member church lamented the fact that he couldn't find enough people to teach Sunday-school classes. 'A crisis is looming,' he told me. 'Soon we won't be able to run a Sunday school at all. All the kids will have to stay in the service for the whole time and people will complain that they're not getting the level of teaching they need to sustain their lives through the week.'

All sorts of issues coalesce around such situations, and teasing them out is a complicated business. But here goes.

You didn't notice I'd gone

It might seem strange, but a good place to start is with why people give up on church altogether. Very few people leave church because they've lost their faith in Jesus. They quit for more prosaic and mundane reasons, but reasons important enough to make them change sometimes quite ingrained habits.

Shaking hands at the door at the end of a service, I was grabbed by a very tall, smartly dressed man with a handle-bar moustache. Almost military in bearing and manner, he congratulated me on what had been a most stimulating sermon. I'd been speaking about God's work around the world, and he had for twenty years been a missionary church-planter in South America. Indeed, he knew one or two of the people I had mentioned in my sermon. He was a visitor at the church and I asked him where he usually worshipped. 'Oh, I don't go to church very often,' he said. 'I don't find much reason to go; no contact between what churches do and what I'm interested in.'

Intrigued, I probed a bit more as people squeezed by us into the night. Didn't he have a lot to contribute to a church in the UK that's declining? 'No-one's interested in what I think or what contribution I could make out of the experience I've had overseas,' he said. I was open-mouthed as he continued. 'I suppose I should give it another go, but it hurts when you're not made welcome.'

It probably hurts even more when, having attended a church for some time, you stop going and no one comes round to find out why. Remember the *Gone but not Forgotten* report mentioned in the Introduction? One of its most stunning conclusions was that 92% of people who left a church were never visited by someone keen to find out the reason.

It's bad enough when people slip through the net and no-one notices that they've gone. It's worse when a minister's attention is drawn to the fact that a family is leaving church because they're unhappy, and the minister's reaction is: 'Well, that's one of those things. It can't be helped.' That hardly endears strugglers to the church.

Early in my pastorate a woman left the church. It was drawn to my attention and I went to visit her. It was not the easiest of encounters. She hadn't liked a sermon I'd preached, didn't really like my style of doing things and indicated that she'd be looking elsewhere. I wished her well in her search and assured her that she'd be welcome to come back, and that if she needed anything in the meantime, she had my number. I wasn't being a super-minister. I was doing my job, as I saw it, of tending the flock God had entrusted to me. She wandered around for a couple of years before returning to our church. I like to think she returned because we left the door open for her to do so.

A declining church cannot afford to lose people, especially people with gifts and energy to contribute, through carelessness or indifference. Often people on the edge of church feel awkward, even excluded. They're not part of the decision-making process and so they often don't feel able either to own or to criticize decisions made and plans adopted by their church. We'll return to this in the next chapter.

One size does not fit all

I spoke to someone the other day who told me that she'd attended a meeting at her church where they'd been asked to do a kind of spiritual health-check. It consisted of a tick-box questionnaire covering such things as 'Do you pray?' 'Is your marriage OK?' 'Are you reading the Bible?' Basically, if you ticked 'yes' to all these questions, you were all right. 'I was aghast,' she told me. 'I assumed there'd be some kind of challenge, some opportunity to explore crucial areas of spirituality and growth. It was like doing a shoppers' survey.'

Among the reasons for leaving church that *Gone but Not Forgotten* unearths is the crucial one of the church's failure to recognize the depth of social change. 'Baby boomers are leaving churches because they find them too much like other institutions and lacking authenticity and credibility; they reject "pre-packaged" religion; they find churches too dogmatic and conformist … they feel stunted by the church in their spiritual and personal growth.'[2] In short, they're looking for a challenge and not finding it. 'Baby busters have extra reasons for leaving churches: they resent being treated as passive consumers; they reject easy answers and any hint of manipulation; and they find that worship is too intellectualised and fails to engage all their senses.'[3]

People quit church not because it's too hard or challenging, but because it appears too easy. Why is this? In his provocative book *The Post-Evangelical*, Dave Tomlinson contrasts 'flat-packs' with Meccano sets. Flat-pack furniture, he says, comes in a box with an instruction sheet. You have to put it together yourself, but you can only make what's pictured on the box. You have no freedom to invent. 'Post-evangelicals', he suggests, 'are more at ease with a Meccano set which still has a basic set of components but which offers you an instruction book full of different possible models which can be constructed – some more basic and others highly elaborate.'[4]

One of the major reasons that people struggle with the church today is its tendency to offer a one-size-fits-all version of Christianity. This is obviously much easier for ministers and leaders who feel stretched and unsupported to run, but at the end of the day it can be counter-productive, as it seems to drive away as many people as it attracts.

In his perceptive analysis of the Alpha phenomenon in the diocese of Lichfield, Mark Ireland comments, 'I am aware of [a] reason why process evangelism courses, and *Alpha* in particular, have caught on so quickly around the diocese. In conversation one incumbent summed it up to me in a single word, "desperation". When faithful clergy have struggled for years to faithfully proclaim the gospel and yet have seen churches inexorably decline, there is a strong temptation to copy a "successful" model that seems to be working elsewhere.'[5]

He's absolutely right. Almost everywhere I go, ministers and church leaders tell me that they're just launching Alpha, or cell church, or purpose-driven leadership, or seeker services – depending on what's been in the Christian press and topping the bestseller lists at Wesley Owen over the past few weeks. None of these things is bad in itself. Indeed, all of them have much to commend them. The problem is that desperate ministers and the churches they lead drop on them as *the* remedy that is going to turn the church around. And who can blame them? After all, in a consumer culture everyone wants a product that works, and pastors who adopt these programmes are able to demonstrate to their churches that they are about to consume a product that has delivered the goods in countless places up and down the land – at least, that's what the hype said on the wrapper.

The problem with this is that many on the margins of the church – and even some close to the centre – feel alienated and excluded by the adoption of such models and practices. The leader of a large Anglican church in the centre of

London, which has hundreds doing an Alpha course on its premises each year, told me that he can't think of one person who has joined the church and got involved in its life and ministry as a result. 'I've mentioned this to the vicar but he told me to stop whinging.'

A committed member of another church lamented that he'd seen so many bandwagons pass through his church over the past decade, he wasn't sure which one he was supposed to be riding any more. 'We were just getting into a programme of seeker services when the Toronto blessing erupted and everything stopped so we could pray,' he says. 'Then it was Alpha and recently we were all encouraged to go to a cell-church conference. These are all great initiatives, but the problem is that we don't have any time at all to think about how we can mould them to our particular situation, to meet the needs of our members and those in the community around us. It's hard not to sound cynical.'

Another leader commented that his church had lost more people over the past decade because the church had chopped and changed so much. 'One person left because she felt church was becoming more like Tesco but not such good value for money,' he said.

These are extreme examples, of course. Many churches have benefited from these initiatives and from others. But sadly, the people who are lost in this process are often those for whom church had already become a struggle because they were failing to find a connection between what happened in church and what was happening in their lives at home, at work and in society at large. And it is these people, often thoughtful and creative, who could form the bridges that churches desperately need to those around them who wouldn't dream of darkening their doors.

Another group who suffer are those whose expectations are raised every time a new initiative is tried, only to have them dashed when the programme didn't quite work as planned.

Disappointment is not a great motivator. People will drift from the centre to the margins of a congregation if they are disappointed too many times, if the church fails to deliver what it promises.

Do you come here often?

One of the first things that frequently happens when people are struggling with church is that their attendance drops off. Time was when committed Christians were all at church twice on Sunday and twice during the week. This dropped to once on Sunday and fortnightly at home group. In many churches this has now dropped to one Sunday in two or three.

Standing on the steps of yet another large and apparently successful church, shaking hands and saying goodbye to people of all ages and races, the minister said to me, 'We have a worshipping community of 350 to 400, but never get more than 200 or so on a given Sunday morning. Many people come every other week or one week in three. So, how do you disciple people? How do you run a preaching series that works its way consecutively through a Bible book or a set of topical or lifestyle issues when people are hearing one in three or four of them? How can you plan home groups when people come to one a month? And don't even start me on how you run weekly things like Sunday school, youth groups, a worship band, etc., etc.'

The fact that people come less frequently often has nothing to do with their level of commitment to Jesus or even to the church. It has everything to do with the demands of the world we live in and the energy levels people have for involvement in yet another demanding activity – church.

Gone are the days when men worked nine to five and had only a short journey home, and women were there waiting for them with the children bathed and a meal on the table, so that by 7pm those men – or their wives if it was their turn – could set off to a church meeting. And those days aren't coming back. Almost all households need two incomes to pay the bills; working days and travelling times have stretched so that both partners are frequently leaving their homes before 7am and not getting back until 8pm. Add children to this picture and it's a wonder anyone anywhere makes it to a midweek meeting.

Many more people than ever are working at weekends, with supermarkets open twenty-four hours a day and most shops open for most of Sunday, call centres operating round the clock, and all kinds of employees, from teachers to computer programmers, project managers to social workers, having to bring work home to finish for Monday morning.

Is the time coming when we have to think seriously about whether a meeting on Sundays at 11am (or whatever time it may be) for everyone in the fellowship is a viable approach to doing church in the twenty-first century? I think it probably is – at least in some communities.

Many of those who in previous generations would have found fulfilment in doing voluntary work for the church – such as leading a youth club or singing in the choir – now find that fulfilment in their working lives. They believe their job is a vocation. The trouble is, when they look to church to resource that vocation, they are disappointed.

Don, a company director, who takes seriously God's calling on him to create wealth and safeguard the livelihoods of those who work for him, looked for support from his minister – only to be told that his attendance record at church was poor and he really needed to get his commitment sorted out. 'I'm committed to ensuring people in my company have safe working conditions, that we don't trash the environment, that our trading practices are just, that I make decisions that are marked by honesty and integrity that everyone at all levels in the company can see,' he said. 'I don't need to be told that I'm letting the side down because I'm not at home group. That's a pressure I can do without.'

People like Don are finding that a small group of like-minded people in similar working situations is actually more of a support to them in their callings than attending church is. Unfortunately, the church is losing their gifts and, more importantly, their contacts with the worlds of work in which so many of the people we are trying to reach with the good news of Jesus find themselves.

Of course, work is not all unalloyed joy. Some people find themselves trapped in one or two low-paid jobs, working all hours just to keep the wolf from the door. Many of these are single mums who could do with having a supportive group of people around them. Mel struggles to make ends meet. A single mum with two primary-age children, she cleans offices for three hours first thing in the morning (which means a 4:30am start), gets the kids off to school and then works in a supermarket until the end of the school day. Jenny and Gordon, a retired couple from her church, often collect the kids, give them tea and cook Mel an evening meal. 'I think I'd go under but for them, you know,' she says. 'When I get a bill I'm not expecting, I sometimes just panic. Gordon helps me budget and sometimes talks to the council for me.'

All this puts pressure on ministers and church leaders to organize programmes flexible enough to meet the needs of people who make demands of church not made in previous generations, and who are available for less than half the time their parents were to have those demands met. No wonder ministerial stress levels are rising and the numbers succumbing to stress-related illnesses seem to be on the rise.

No-one knows the story any more

This brings us to what I suspect is the deepest part of the hole in which the church currently finds itself. In the Introduction, we referred to the loss of the Christian story in our culture. Time was when everyone in Britain saw the world in roughly the same way. We believed that certain things were right and other things were wrong. We were optimistic, believing that things would get better and that good would triumph over evil. This view of life was based on centuries of exposure to the Christian story through school, church, the legal system, the art we looked at and the books we read.

Describing why over 3 million people came to hear Billy Graham in the 1950s, Callum Brown says: 'The mental world which drew in those worshippers was a national culture, widely broadcast through books, magazines and radio and deeply ingrained in the rhetoric with which people conversed about each other and about themselves. It was a world profoundly conservative in morals and outlook, and fastidious in its adherence to respectability and moral standards.'[6] Not everyone bought into Billy Graham, but few fundamentally disagreed with what he stood for. And so, 'During the late 1940s and the first half of the 1950s, organized Christianity experienced the greatest per annum growth in church membership ... since the eighteenth century.'[7]

'Then, really quite suddenly in 1963, something very profound ruptured the character of the nation and its people, sending organized Christianity on a downward spiral to the margins of social significance.'[8] People left church, stopped sending their children to Sunday school and at a profound level ceased to see the world in the way they and their parents and their grandparents had seen it for generations. The Christian story was no longer the favoured explanation for life, the universe and everything.

Brown's explanation for this is that the 1960s was the decade when all the tenets of the Enlightenment project finally crashed down around our ears. We ceased to believe in progress, began to question whether science brought only benefits, stopped accepting what our elders and betters said and started to explore new ideas and stories that had been around for a while but which hadn't been regarded as respectable. The 1960s opened with protests about nuclear weapons, the collapse of censorship following the Lady Chatterley trial and the eruption of teen culture and rock n' roll. It closed with riots, flower power, feminism, the legalization of abortion and homosexuality and the widespread acceptance that lifestyles and morals were matters of personal choice.

Whether we accept all the details of Brown's argument or not, there's no denying the truth of his central case: Christianity in Britain collapsed in a very short space of time; the church is now marginal to the lives of most people, who no longer know, let alone believe, the Christian story. But many in our churches are still shell-shocked. They just haven't come to terms with this seismic change.

When I'm leading a service in their church I often ask people to describe how the world has changed since they were children. The over-fifties almost invariably answer by lamenting the lack of faith and morals in our society. I sometimes respond by asking whether our culture is immoral or just operating to a different set of moral principles from the ones Christians operate by. In response, one woman told me bluntly that the problem is that 'too many people think for themselves these days and don't do as they're told'.

As a historian, Brown does not think this situation could ever be reversed – though whether historians should get into prophecy is a moot point. His reason for saying this, however, is worth hearing: 'If the argument of this book is correct,' he says, 'missions of the new millennium will fail amongst the young because of their unfamiliarity with discursive Christianity due to its disappearance from the family and youth media, and the young's absence from Sunday Schools.'[9]

His view was echoed by Mark Santer, Bishop of Birmingham, on Radio 4's *Today* programme. 'We are confirming older people who have residual memory of Sunday school,' he said. 'The children of the sixties and seventies who did not go to Sunday school will not have that residual memory when they are in their fifties.' This chimes in with research from the States suggesting that the rapid growth of churches such as Willow Creek and Saddleback happened because they were appealing to the used-to-be-churched and presented the faith in a new and more relevant way. It suggests that evangelism might get harder rather than easier.

There seem to me to be two major responses to this changed situation – neither of which looks like a goer in the long term. The first, which we've already talked about, is trying lots of new ideas – seeker services, Alpha, cell church and the like – to reverse the decline in attendance. As I said before, each of these initiatives has great potential for the thinking church. But each of them assumes an audience for our message that is familiar with and interested in the Christian story. 'Seeker services are a good example of the church trying to be relevant but succeeding in being relevant only to itself,' says Barry Linney. 'Rather than listening to those outside, we were still only speaking to them after listening to our own heartbeat.'[10]

The second is to come over all nostalgic for the time when the churches were full and Christians set the moral agenda for the nation, and to put all our eggs in the revival basket. Now, I want to see people finding faith in Jesus and joining the church – that's the whole reason for this book. But I do not believe that revival is a quick fix for the hole in which we find ourselves.

The great strength of the Christian church over the centuries is that it has adapted to cultures all over the world, so that people can hear the Christian message in a way that they can understand and respond to. This is why the church in Nepal and the church in Brazil are different from each other in terms of organization and social practice. But both are growing hand over fist, and perhaps one reason for this is that in both countries the church operates at the margins of society, among the poor and those who do not set the cultural agenda. The challenge for us is not how quickly we can turn the clock back to when we were top dogs, but how we can adapt what we do and say to the new culture of the twenty-first century.

There is a danger that, having lost ground so quickly, the church becomes defensive and prickly, we pull up the drawbridge, circle the wagons and let in only those who see things exactly as we do. If we do this, we'll disappear just as surely as the church in Antioch crashed out of existence in the early seventh century, having been the most significant force in the expansion of Christianity for half a millennium.

To sum up, we've identified seven issues that the church struggles with: it can be careless about people on the edge or those who have just left it; it doesn't offer enough challenge and stimulation; it assumes that a one-size-fits-all faith will suit everyone who comes; it is prone to leap on bandwagons which can raise expectations and then leave people disappointed and disillusioned; it's failing to adapt to social changes that mean that even committed people attend less frequently; it hasn't come to terms with changes in the world of work; and it's trying to minister in a culture that no longer has the faintest idea what the church is talking about.

Are these reasons to feel gloomy, or what? I don't think so.

I wouldn't start from here

You've heard the joke about the motorist who finds himself lost in the depths of the countryside, stops, winds down his window and asks a local leaning on a farm gate how to get to his destination. 'Ah,' replies the local. 'If I were you, I wouldn't start from here.'

If we were starting the church from scratch, we certainly would not start from where we are now after 2,000 years of sometimes glorious, sometimes ignominious existence. We'd start with a clean sheet, unencumbered by our history, our institutions, our traditions and ways of doing things. After all, we're not just in a culture that isn't Christian, as many missionaries are; we're in a culture that tried Christianity, found it wanting and rejected it. Many people, especially those under fifty, feel that the church was responsible for sanctioning western colonialism, the ecological crisis and the exploitation of women. And, however unfairly, they aren't about to give it another chance.

At the same time, many in our culture are looking for a spirituality that works, and, when introduced to Jesus as though for the first time, are drawn to him, intrigued by what he stood for and how he lived, attracted to his powerful critique of the prevailing social order and care of the marginalized, inspired by his hope in a future that's better, more just and peaceful than any present we've ever known.

And one of the best ways to introduce people to this Jesus is through involvement in our communities. Over the past twenty years the church has rediscovered its rich heritage of social action. All over the place churches are running parent and toddler groups; drop-in centres for families, drug addicts, the unemployed and those with mental-health problems; lunch clubs for the elderly; adult literacy classes and language courses for refugees and other immigrants.

This is happening for two reasons. One is that the church has rediscovered that social action is part of the gospel. It's what Jesus did (see Luke 5:12 – 6:11) and it's how the early Christians demonstrated God's love to a pagan world.[11] And the second is that in very many areas of the UK the church is actually the only functioning part of the voluntary sector, and so government – both local and national – is looking to the churches to provide services for their communities in a way that the statutory sector cannot.[12]

So does the church have any role to play in helping such people to encounter Jesus? Michael Green says an unequivocal 'yes'. 'Wherever Christianity has been at its most healthy, evangelism has stemmed from the local church, and has had a noticeable impact on the surrounding area. I do not believe that the re-Christianisation of the West can take place without the renewal of local churches in this whole area of evangelism.'[13] Veteran church-watcher David Edwards offers a more nuanced view: 'Because the decline of the churches has been so substantial … it seems likely that for most of the English what survives of Christianity will continue to be more or less churchless, unless churches become radically different.'[14]

And the authors of *The Prodigal Project* assert: 'This book is not anti-church. If anything it is a call to renew our hope in what the church might yet become. We want to grab the attention of those drifting toward the fringes of the established church (or already beyond it) and suggest that giving up may be premature. We hope to persuade any who will hear that the current crisis of the church in the West is a time of great opportunity, and that underneath all the anxiety and discomfort there is the hint of God's restless stirring.'[15]

I believe that too. Furthermore, I believe that ministers and leaders of churches, and those drifting to the edge of church and beyond, need to come together and talk and work for a future for the church that will enable those being tossed around in the sea of cultural change and uncertainty to find safety, belonging, challenge and hope aboard God's only lifeboat in this world – the church.

8 Subverting the church for good

'This is what I reckon, for what it's worth,' said Max, who was currently, as he put it, 'between congregations'. 'I put in a lot of hours at my last church before I realized that I was just furthering the career of the minister.'

Ouch. Given my job at the time, I didn't think it my place to argue. I'm sure it's the case that churches can seem to be ministerial fiefdoms, leaving their members feeling like serfs contributing to another's personal development but starving their own. Of course, if you talk to a group of ministers, the chances are that they'll tell you the reverse – poor salaries, demanding congregations, long hours, high burnout rates, trouble with members, trouble with colleagues …

That was Colin's story. He rang. 'It's all happening tonight,' he said. 'The deacons have finally decided they've got to lance the boil.'

You remember Colin? We met him in the first chapter. He was a minister struggling with his church because of the actions of a senior colleague. Now the waste matter was about to hit the air-conditioning, and he felt a mixture of angst and anticipation. 'It could go one of two ways,' he said, rather obviously. 'Either he'll come clean and we'll get it all out into the open, and we can move forward. Or he'll continue to brazen it out and it'll get very ugly.'

In the event, Colin's senior colleague made a partial admission of what had been happening in his life, apologized to the church, and acknowledged that in some ways he'd let them all down. People felt a mixture of shock and relief – shock that such things were going on under their noses; relief because most people felt something was wrong, and now that it was out in the open it could be dealt with. Of course, it wasn't the end of the affair. The church had to work through the pain of the situation, decide what had to be done, and chart a way forward. And because the senior minister had not come clean about everything, tensions remained. In the event – and for very different reasons – both Colin and his colleague left their jobs at the church not long afterwards. No-one ever said being honest with one another would be easy.

And the church still hasn't recovered. A new minister has come and gone. The church has lost its way a bit. Some former leaders have quit for other congregations. People have fallen out over the direction the church should be taking. Saddest of all, its struggles have unsettled the faith of many, and a good few have given up church altogether as a result. They were looking for a fellowship that would resource their lives in the world. What they got was a church riven with in-fighting, where ministerial unfaithfulness left open wounds seemingly too deep to heal.

Life at church is a bed of roses. Its beauty can leave you stunned. Its thorns can tear you to pieces. Life in it is a mixture of the two; one hopes that the beauty outweighs the blood loss. In previous chapters we've seen what the church is, what it's for, why it's important to join one if we want to follow Jesus and how the church in Britain is itself struggling to come to terms with the new situation it finds itself in.

In this chapter we're going to look at how we go about getting involved in church in such a way as to maximize the benefits and minimize the pain; how we ensure that involvement is not about building ministerial careers or ecclesiastical empires, but about extending the kingdom of God. And we're going to see how church can be a vital springboard to effective life and action in the big wide world God has called us to live in – because, after all, that's the arena in which the kingdom of God needs to be making its major impact.

Don't cramp my style

'I wish he'd realize I have a life during the week,' said Corine. We'd met at a lunch for Christians in business. She was off to a meeting with overseas clients and then out with colleagues to relax. 'The trouble is, I can't be in two places at once, and if I choose to go with my colleagues to this show, I can't be at home group. And if I'm not at home group, I get it in the neck on Sunday. If I don't go to the show I miss a golden opportunity to get to know the people I work with better. What am I supposed to do? And why can't I talk about this with people at my church?' Breathless, she was gone.

Corine is not unique. Many of us, as we saw in the previous chapter, feel pulled in opposite directions by the demands of work and the expectations of church. When you add to that the responsibilities we have to our families and to ourselves – to eat properly, keep fit, have fun and sleep – it's little wonder that at times we feel like tearing our hair out.

'I've lost count of the number of times I've been snubbed,' said William. 'I've got something to contribute here that I and other people think we need, but the leaders aren't interested. I don't know how much longer I'll stick it out.'

I sympathized with him. I remember when I was an enthusiastic twentysomething journalist, keen to contribute to church life. My minister, a good and godly man, told a group of us that while he was quite willing to involve us in the service, none of us could preach or plan the whole thing. 'After all,' he said, 'I can write, but I don't try to do Simon's job.' We were too crestfallen to argue with such flawed logic. Some of us wondered how long we'd stick it out. I wonder if I ever cramped someone's enthusiasm when I was their pastor.

'I love being involved. It's just that I need a break,' said Paul. 'I've been doing this role for four or five years, and I'd like a change. But I'm getting the vibe that I'm letting the side down by even thinking about taking a break.'

I'm sure many of us have been there: started doing something at our church – often to help out when people were thin on the ground – and five years later found ourselves stuck in the role that feels like a straitjacket, because the church is too inflexible to release us to do something else.

And then there's Colin's church. How many of us have been wounded by the failure of a Christian leader to live up to his calling? I have. The disappointment cuts deep and lasts a long time. And yet why are we surprised that leaders fall? They are only flesh and blood like us, prone to the same temptations that we are and thus needing the same levels of support that we do. But as we saw in chapter 1, some church leaders act as though they've got it taped and sorted and they never make mistakes. If only!

'The problem with evangelicalism in the West is not its lack of intellectual credibility,' says Carl Trueman: 'rather, it is its frequent lack of moral integrity, its tendency towards materialism, and its lip-service to a doctrinal tradition and a code of ethics, sexual and social, which it often despises and ignores in practice – and this lack of honesty and integrity is the responsibility of each and every one of us.'[1] How true. He adds: 'we live in a kind of simplistic evangelical culture where people are not meant to have certain problems. We pay lip-service to all being sinners, but we cannot imagine that any Christian would actually be involved in any serious public sin, such as embezzlement or adultery.'[2]

And churches are reluctant to talk publicly about ministers who have sex with other men's wives, or youth leaders who abuse children, or treasurers who rip off church funds. Naturally, we don't want to broadcast such stories, as though we gloried in them like the tabloid press. Neither do we want to fuel our seemingly insatiable appetite for salacious gossip. But surely, if we care about one another we'll want to cultivate a culture of grace in our churches that will enable us to talk about these things without being prurient or judgmental.

'When I think of friends who have fallen,' says Trueman, 'I feel guilty, not just because they did not feel able to ask me for help, but also because I failed to tell them the gospel as often as I should have done.'[3] Of course, such honesty comes at a price: we cannot open up to someone we hardly know. Trueman suggests that we should be confessing our sins to one another (James 5:16). This demands that we forge deep, close and open relationships with one another. This is costly. It is time-consuming. But it's what the church should be good at, because each of us is buoyed up by grace.

Yes, church truly is a bed of roses – I've got the scars to prove it. Being part of any community, of course, involves give and take on both sides. When we join a church, we change it, and we have the potential to change it much more than we think. But equally, whenever we join something, we are changed by the new relationships we've entered into. The trick is ensuring that the benefits outweigh the costs on both sides.

So how do we go about it? I have three suggestions. I offer them tentatively, and ask you to work out for yourself how they might apply in your situation. Even better, talk them over with friends and formulate your own strategies for getting the most out of church and giving the best you can to it. First up is *commitment*.

Commitment v. commitments

The generation growing up behind me is referred to by various epithets (some of them polite). The least attractive is 'slacker generation'. It implies that people born in the prosperous 1960s, who grew up in the troubled 1970s, have a problem with commitment. It's hardly surprising in one sense. After all, this is the generation that matured in the shadow of the killing fields of Vietnam and the abortion clinic; a generation that knew unparalleled prosperity but received precious little guidance about how to cope with it; a generation that had everything it wanted but nothing it really needed. And so, the pundits say, it's a group of slackers, drifting in search of values to live by.

This is an unfair picture, however. You have only to look at the commitment of this generation to issues of Third World development and environmental protection to recognize a passion for justice sadly lacking in many of their forebears. And you have only to think that this generation provided the inspiration, nous and energy for the explosion of the computer and communications industries, which are transforming the globe beyond recognition, to realize that this is not a value-free, comatose, demographic blip.

It is, however, a generation that has rewritten the rules about joining in. It has questioned the institutions that have run our society for so long, such as trade unions, political parties and the like (as we saw in chapter 1). Unlike the baby-boomers, who thought collective action could change the world and that it was cool to participate and sing with strangers, this generation has prized individual freedom above everything, and asked 'Why?' Its attitude to institutions is raising for all of us, whatever our age, the whole issue of commitment to the church.

I've talked to retired people who struggle to commit themselves to a church they see drifting from them. 'It's all for the young – guitars, overhead projectors, ministers in jeans and drama and dance in the sanctuary.' Molly was a committed member of her church but now feels that it doesn't meet her needs at all. Like many people a quarter her age who've given her permission to do so, she's asking, 'What's the point?'

One Christmas, in our church, we planned a modestly ambitious programme of events to communicate the good news of the coming of Jesus in a fun, outsider-friendly way. One Saturday, we decked out the church hall for a family party, bought in the nibbles and drinks, planned the games and waited for the punters. The fog descended and no-one came. We blamed the weather. Other events, however, also flopped and we began to blame ourselves.

By the following spring, it felt as though a spirit of torpor had descended on us like the fog that wiped out our Christmas event. I was told by a number of church members that I needed to preach on commitment. One longstanding leader, a woman well over retirement age, was strident in her opinion: 'God isn't blessing us', she said, 'because we are not giving our all to him. People are putting other things before their commitment to the Lord's work here.' It was a temptingly obvious explanation of our difficulties. People were not turning up in the sort of numbers we had come to expect; it must be because they were growing lukewarm. Someone even suggested I preach on the church in Laodicea, which Jesus threatens to spew from his mouth like a lukewarm drink (Revelation 3).

I was troubled. Instead of lecturing I resorted to listening. *Why* were people not coming to planned events? We talked about it as we sat around the table at Rory and Alice's flat one Friday evening. He was a twentysomething designer working for a small consultancy specializing in retail design, and had been in three European countries that week, working with clients. Alice, also a designer, was stuck in an increasingly demanding and unrewarding job. They'd helped to build our church up from a tiny gathering to a vibrant community of more than fifty committed members, but had recently stepped down from leading a home group.

In the course of our conversation it became clear that their commitment to Jesus and to his people in this area was undiminished. What had changed was the economy. Work for Rory's business was harder to come by in the UK, hence the level of international travel. The hours he was having to put in were rising because the company couldn't afford to take on extra staff to meet extra demand. Rory's energy was being consumed by the career he believed God had called him into. New openings for Alice were non-existent, and her energy and *joie de vivre* were being sapped. Neither had a lot of get-up-and-go left over for organizing church activities in the evenings or at weekends.

Other people had similar stories to tell. Most of our members had jobs, but those jobs were becoming more demanding as the business world became tougher and companies struggled to stay afloat in ever more competitive markets. People were being expected to work longer hours with fewer colleagues. One friend spoke of the stresses this was introducing into his home life for the first time in over twenty years of marriage. Danny, my electrician friend, found himself having to work nights and Sundays because the only job his firm had for him was rewiring a shopping centre in London's West End. Others complained of being more stretched, more harassed and more tired than they'd ever been. Church suffered.

That spring I was preaching through John's Gospel. Time and again we came up against texts that urged us to be faithful to what God had called us to. It forced us as a church to look at what we ought to be committed to, what we ought to be expecting people to commit themselves to, and how we ought to arrange our support for one another so that we could help one another keep our commitments. We're still working on it.

Committed to what?

It forced me to think about what I thought God expected of people. I became convinced that Max was right. Some church leaders call for commitment from their members because it helps them to build a church, a ministry, a reputation, a career. That is not what Jesus is asking us to commit ourselves to. But I was certain that God was calling us to be committed to one another. We are a family. We need one another. When the going gets tough, the tough get help. And that help ought to come from our brothers and sisters. So we need to be committed to church.

Reading John's Gospel together also helped us to focus on the things that mattered to Jesus. It particularly turned our attention from ourselves to the world around us, and encouraged us to find God and our primary sphere of service there, rather than within the four walls of our church building. It was helpful for a number of reasons.

For one thing, we were in the throes of embarking on a project to provide daycare for people with mental-health problems living in our community, in partnership with the local psychiatric hospital. For another, it helped our members to see their workplaces as a primary location for their ministry. And it also did wonders for our church football team, with a number of blokes deciding that kicking an inflated pig's bladder around on a Tuesday night could be a valuable ministry. They were right. Half the team were not Christians, so our guys were not only getting fit, they were also forming friendships with people who needed to hear about Jesus. But, of course, it meant that few of them made it to church activities on a Wednesday.

When we talk about commitment at church, we need to be very clear what we are calling people to be committed to. Jesus said, 'Follow me.' When he filled that out, it was with a word about catching people rather than serving on committees. Of course there are committees to be served on. (Whether there have to be quite so many is a moot point!) And there are jobs to be done to ensure that the church can actually be what God wants it to be. Small-group leaders, teachers, people to look after children, musicians, painters, administrators, gardeners, builders, carpenters – you name it, the church needs it. (Of course, this presupposes the church as currently constituted. Later in the chapter we'll ask ourselves whether church actually has to be this way for everyone.)

But the work of the kingdom of God requires that there be Christian electricians, estate agents, bankers, social workers, carpenters, plumbers, shop workers, and so on – people pursuing their careers as a calling from God, faithful in developing and using the skills he's given them for his glory. He calls us to be committed to our work. It is our worship (as we saw in chapter 2). For years, the church has been dogged by an unhealthy split between the sacred (what we do on Sundays and Wednesday evenings) and the secular (what we do during the rest of the time). I once heard a preacher say that we work only to earn money to invest in church work, and that we should use our energies to serve not our employers during the day but our churches during the evenings and at weekends. This is a travesty of what the Bible says. Time and again Scripture calls us to live out our faith in the world of work, community-building, the arts and politics. As we saw in chapter 2, the primary purpose of meeting together on Sunday is that we'll be better equipped to worship in our workplace on Monday.

So we have to make choices. If we commit ourselves to being at home group on Wednesday, we can't be at the residents' association meeting, and *vice versa*. If we commit ourselves to work on the missionary committee, we cannot go for a meal with our work colleagues on the same night, and *vice versa*. One is not better, more worthwhile or more spiritual than the other. What we have to decide is where God wants us to be. And we need each other's help and the church's support in making and sticking to those decisions.

This became an acute issue for the band Delirious. Based in Littlehampton, the five-piece led worship and did evangelism locally. Slowly, they evolved into a fully fledged pop band with a chart single and album getting serious attention from the mainstream music press. They had a choice. Lead singer Martin Smith said it was something that the band constantly talked about. 'How can you be in a rock 'n' roll band and be a good husband and a good dad?' he asked. 'There are times when I'm away and times when I'm at home, it's something we've all had to adjust to. But we're all in church with our wives and families most Sundays. I can honestly say that the family thing is still our priority, although there is a season right now where we're having to work really hard.'[4]

Smith and his colleagues had to make choices. We all do. And we need one another's help. One Sunday I found myself sitting next to Jim at church. After the service we talked about how things were going and he said he was finding juggling his commitments a struggle. He outlined what he was involved in at work, home and church, and then said, 'I know I'm doing too much, but I can't help it. Work is piling the pressure on and church is as demanding of me as it always is. What can I do?' He said that every time he thought about giving up a church commitment, he felt guilty. I suggested that being able to do one or two things well at church was better than doing half a dozen badly. He agreed, but said he didn't know what he could drop.

So we made a list of what he was doing at church and ranked them according to how fulfilling he found each task, which he was most gifted for, and which was the most important in the life of the church – important generally, and important that he do it rather than someone else. He remarked that it didn't seem very spiritual. But I suggested that it might just save him from having a nervous breakdown.

It does no harm for all of us to try a similar exercise. We need to ask a series of questions about what we're doing in church and whether we're gifted for it. What are our gifts? What are we good at? Is what we're doing in church making the best use of the talents God has given us? Then we need to ask ourselves about our other commitments – work, home, family, community. And finally we need to ask ourselves how much time we have got to devote to the various parts of our life. The answer to this question will change over time. People who are single and living alone may have more time for outside activities than those who are married with very young children. Retired people whose children are all living away from home may have more time than an area manager or site foreman with children at secondary school.

It is always good to do this exercise with someone else. This will help us to be more objective and realistic – both about our gifts and talents, and about how much time we have for church activities. Often, talking these issues over with another person enables us to identify strengths we didn't know we had, and gives us strategies for overcoming weaknesses we were only too well aware of but were seemingly powerless to do anything about.

Not everyone agrees that this is the way forward. Phil Hill argues: 'The consumer society has invaded the church. We go to take what we want from it rather than give it what it needs, either in money or personal involvement. Highly capable people withhold their gifts from church on the basis of the pressures they face through home and work. Even when they do offer to serve, their criterion for working is not that it fulfils the church's mission but that it fulfils the person's desire for achievement or desire to serve.'[5]

Hill clearly hankers after simpler times. Earlier in his book he waxed lyrical about going to church on Sunday morning, afternoon and evening. The trouble with such advice is that it only makes people like Don or Mel – whom we met in the last chapter – feel torn and guilty, and could well push them out of church altogether. He's right, of course, that some people hang back from committing themselves to church for all the wrong reasons, and he affirms that Christians need to be involved in the world, acting as salt and light.[6] I just wonder whether he remains wedded to a model of the church that worked in the modern world but will not cut the mustard in the postmodern one. We'll return to this.

Choosing a family

One of the choices most of us who are Christians feel we ought to make is to give church a go. Jackie told me of her struggles with church that led to her leaving. 'I don't feel right not going to worship God on a Sunday morning,' she said. 'There's something missing from life.' She resolved to look for another church. This is never easy. Whether we've recently moved to a new area, or have had to leave our old church for some other reason, finding a new Christian family is never straightforward.

Most of us know what we're looking for, based on experiences we've had, both good and bad. We know that we want a church where we'll be made to feel welcome; where we'll make friends, find lots of people our own age (including several who do similar jobs), and discover that the church is praying for someone with just our mixture of gifts to join them. Yeah, dream on! Chances are that we'll pitch up at a place on a Sunday morning when the minister is away on holiday, the person greeting folk on the door had a trying week and a row with his kids that morning, the worship group is depleted by flu, and the preacher is not exactly firing on all cylinders. We have a choice: leave and shake the dust from our feet, or give it a number of Sundays before we write it off or get stuck in.

Remember Mary from chapter 1? Sunday after Sunday she came to our church. Sunday after Sunday no-one spoke to her or made her feel welcome. The only reason she stayed was that no-one told her not to come! She stuck it out, persevering through the pig ignorance of others until she made a mark on the church that is deep and indelible. Not everyone has the personal resources and willpower to do that. But we ought to give it a go. One way of making it easier is to latch on to a welcoming face, make a beeline for that person each Sunday and ask him or her to introduce us to other people.

All of us who are comfortably ensconced in our churches need to be aware of newcomers, and go out of our way to say hello and make them feel welcome – even if it means leaving off talking to a friend in order to speak to a stranger. Church leaders and ministers should model this behaviour. Churches should also think about establishing a team whose special responsibility it is to spot new people and make them welcome. If strangers don't stick, nine times out of ten it isn't their fault; it's ours, for not opening our circle and drawing them in.

This is much easier, of course, in a smaller group than a large one. New research carried out by Peter Brierley for the Archbishop of Canterbury's Springboard initiative found that large churches are declining faster than small ones. Apparently, the figures shocked Anglican bigwigs, but I'd have thought they were a statement of the obvious. Newcomers are nearly always noticed and made welcome in a small church but missed in a large one. Now, however, we have the statistics to back this up. 'More than 70 per cent of churches with at least 200 worshippers show decline, while almost 60 per cent of churches with fewer than 10 worshippers show growth.'[7]

Smaller gatherings are generally less formal than big meetings and thus more able to offer the three characteristics that Mark Ireland suggests are the key to attracting and keeping people: 'A warm and welcoming environment perhaps with a meal, so that belonging can come before believing; high quality biblical teaching with a well thought out and balanced syllabus; and small group discussion with sensitive leadership, enabling people to feel secure enough to ask anything at all.'[8]

Again, such ingredients seem obvious, but ask yourself: does my church offer this as part of the regular programme? It is one of the reasons many large churches are adopting cell-church models and encouraging their members to see the cell as their basic church commitment. At their best, cells offer all three ingredients outlined by Ireland. And they make it possible for the sort of relationships to develop that Carl Trueman was talking about if we are going to be able to guard one another's Christian walk.

Think about it

Commitment is necessary if we're going to make church work. So is what I call *critical belonging*. This doesn't mean carping about everybody's imperfections and railing against the fact that the church isn't heaven. We should remember the beam in our own eye before we list the specks in our brothers' and sisters' eyes. But Jesus doesn't want us to be cabbages. Church is not the ecclesiastical equivalent of the Red Army or Hitler Youth, where lots of unthinking clones do what they're told and, when asked to jump, ask only 'How high?' We need to bring all our critical faculties to bear on our belonging. It is this that has the potential to make church such a rewarding experience. And it is this that could ensure that struggling churches, and Christians on the edge of them who are trying to find a home, could create communities that work for both.

Karen challenged her minister on the issue of what women were allowed to do in church. It seemed that all the opportunities open to females had to do with the kitchen, and the only time they were allowed near the pulpit was to change the flowers and the water for the preacher. This did not square with Karen's reading of Scripture. So instead of walking out, and having talked about it to a number of friends, she asked if she could chat to her minister about it. What ensued was a stormy but fruitful dialogue that led to real change. Things aren't perfect – they never are in church – but they're moving in the right direction.

Tom wanted to get involved in social action, but his church didn't do that sort of thing. Instead of leaving, he asked why it didn't, and discovered that a number of members felt the way he did. Together they did some thinking and Bible study, came up with a plan, and went to see the minister. Several church meetings later – after lots of heated discussion and near fallings-out – the church set up a parents and toddlers group. It grew into a drop-in for families in need, dealing with issues of debt, child discipline and marriage pressure.

We need to be thoughtfully exploring ways of working out our faith and discipleship in the community of God's people we belong to. Jesus spoke to the crowds in parables. Partly this was to avoid being arrested, because his message of the coming kingdom of God – which seemed to exclude Herod Antipas and the Jerusalem hierarchy, not to mention the Romans – was political dynamite. But it was also to tease his hearers into more thoughtful listening. For instance, after he delivered the deceptively simple parable of the sower, his disciples came and asked him what it meant. He commended them for doing so. 'Nothing is hidden that will not be disclosed, nor is anything secret that will not become known and come to light,' he said. 'Then pay attention to how you listen; for to those who have, more will be given' (Luke 8:17–18). Jesus was talking about the kingdom of God and saying that there's no big secret, you've just got to approach it intelligently, listen intently (which means asking questions and thinking about what's being said) and commit yourself to the message so that it changes your life. Interestingly, he said that this can happen only in a group that functions as a family for us – a place where we're supported in our questioning, probing and listening to the Word of God (Luke 8:19–21).

Churches are not cabbage farms where people are supposed to sit mindlessly and passively in rows. Churches need to be places where people ask questions, seek to do things in new ways, and explore together what it means to be the people of

God. While we find security and a sense of belonging at church, church should not be a safe place in the sense that nothing unpredictable, exciting or out of the ordinary happens. After all, church is the dwelling-place of the extraordinary God, who is the Father of our Lord Jesus and who is present in our gathering by his Holy Spirit. It really should not be anodyne and dull.

Some churches are impenetrable. They are run as fiefdoms by ministers and leaders who don't want members who ask questions. Once I spoke to a bookshop manager who didn't like something in the magazine I was editing at the time, so she wasn't going to stock it. When asked if it wasn't up to her customers whether they bought and read the magazine, she replied that her customers got what she allowed them to have. Well, 'Shop somewhere else' is my advice! Unfortunately, there are churches like this, and they are hard to belong to because there is no freedom of thought and movement.

Mercifully, such churches are few and far between. Most ministers and leaders are only too happy to welcome people with ideas and imagination. The trick is matching what needs to be done with the gifts of the people available to do things. This will inevitably involve compromise on both sides.

In order for churches (as they are currently constituted) to function, certain things have to happen – music, preaching, Sunday school, cleaning, maintenance of the building, outreach to the community. But there are lots of ways of ensuring that these things happen. So there is scope for flexibility which allows for peoples' gifts, ideas and creativity to be used.

But this is not the only biblical or viable model of church. We've talked about cell church a couple of times already. Other small-group models might be even better matched to the needs of the emerging culture. One church I know of meets midweek and always shares a meal. It is led by a theologically trained lay-person, so has very low running costs. It suits the needs of the people who go to it. Other similar groups meet all over the country in rural, suburban and inner-city locations.[9]

But such groups are not for everyone. Some people like to worship in the relative anonymity of a large gathering. This is why attendance at cathedral services rose so steeply through the 1990s. Having bathed in the liturgy or jumped to the kicking music of a Soul Survivor-style celebration, such people can get their small-group experience among friends who might or might not worship at the same venue.

In our previous chapter, we identified the tendency of churches to offer a one-size-fits-all spirituality. Some are happy with this – assuming that what's on offer fits them. But most are not. God has created us unique and diverse, and the point of the gospel is that it brings a rich diversity of people together in Christ. This doesn't need to be a crowd, but it oughtn't to be a monochrome set. One of the more interesting and unexpected findings of the Springboard research is that 'Churches with congregations aged entirely under 45 or those with people aged entirely over 45 were … declining, as were all-white congregations … The report says churches do best with a full age spread, tilted toward the younger end, with a wide ethnic mix.'[10] This is what we argued in chapters 3 and 4.

The point is that many churches are struggling to find a way forward in the perplexing new world of the twenty-first century, while many Christians are keen to find a home that meets their needs and uses their gifts, while supporting them in their lives outside church. Critical belonging in these circumstances could lead to thrashing out exciting new ways of being church in the most unlikely of situations.

For instance, Pete found that a number of shift workers weren't able to make any of the meetings his church held – either on Sundays or midweek. They talked about how the church could create a programme that would provide them with fellowship and teaching. The result was a peripatetic home group that meets at different times and in different places through the week. Not rocket science, but many have stuck in the church and brought their friends along as a result.

Make the best use of yourself

Building on critical belonging, the third thing we need in order to make sure we get the best out of church, and that church gets the best out of us, is *creative participation*. We are busy people. Work and family require our attention and energy. But we can allocate some of our time and energy to church. Remember that everything we do is worship, so I'm not suggesting that in deciding how much time we've got to devote to church, we are limiting our commitment to God and his work. Far from it. I am suggesting that we make the most creative allocation of our time and energy that we can.

This brings us back to the theme of gifts. What are my gifts? This question paralyses some Christians because they have a very limited view of gifts. 'I don't speak in tongues, see pictures or bring words of prophecy,' they say, 'so I haven't got any gifts.' This, however, is a dangerously narrow view. God ensures that there are people with the gifts, abilities, talents, and skills to do all the work he wants a particular church to do.

This requires the minister or ministers, the leaders and the members to be creatively listening for and thinking about what God want us to be doing in our church. This involves examining the kind of neighbourhood our church is in, what its needs are, what kind of people come to the church, and what their needs are. Then we need to discover what gifts God has sown among us. This can be an exciting, creative time as we help one another to identify our gifts, skills and abilities. Add to this the interests and community links that various members have, and you have the pointers to an exhilarating voyage of discovery as together you discern what God wants you (as a group) to do in your community, and also what God wants each of you (as individuals) to do to bring the group vision to fruition.

And so we're back considering the shape of the church. Ministers and leaders can often be so caught up in running the institution that they fail to notice that it no longer scratches where people are itching. If we invite all our people to particip- ate creatively in our church, then we've got to be prepared to change the way we do things.

And I don't mean tinker at the edges. People are giving up on the church because it doesn't seem to be flexible enough to meet the challenges of the world we're in. They aren't going to stay because we carpet the sanctuary or start using PowerPoint in the services. They might stay if we abandon meeting on Sunday because it's actually better for everyone to meet during the week in local pubs near where they live. They might stay if ministers commit themselves to allowing their members to set their preaching agendas for half the year. They might stay if the church opens its doors to those in need in its neighbourhood and offered them a chance to get stuck into some kind of ministry among them.

They might stay if a whole lot of things happen. But nothing will happen if church leaders dictate the rules of engagement and church members feel they can't participate in a way that uses their gifts and meets their needs. And nothing will happen if we say that the church in 2020 has to be recog- nizably the same as the church in 1950. After all, no member of Paul's Corinth congregation would recognize what passes for church in the West today.

Let's be under no illusion that this will be easy. Nothing worthwhile is easy. We live in an instant age where everything is on tap and accessible at the push of a button. But instant coffee has nothing of the flavour of fresh ground coffee that takes a little more time and effort to prepare. Likewise with church. Solutions and visions that take effort, imagination and hard work are infinitely rewarding.

Caught up in God's community

A final word. Our commitment, critical belonging and creative participation are worthwhile only because we are caught up in the work of the kingdom of God. We're not interested in personal empires (even our own) or ecclesiastical enterprises that get written up in the magazines and best-sellers. We're interested in the kingdom of God. That's what Jesus came to proclaim and inaugurate. That's what he is working to build through his powerful Spirit in our fallen world.

Church and our commitment to it must therefore be outward-looking. Our imagination and hard work should not be dissipated on structures and organizations that merely do us good or make us feel important. They are too precious for that. God has given us our gifts to build a community that reaches out into our needy world and joins God in his major project of restoration. The whole creation is groaning, longing for the liberty from the bondage to which it has been subjected because of human sin (Romans 8). The church is an agent in God's strategy to redeem the world and to restore what sin has marred, scarred and wrecked.

It is the most exciting thing in the world to be caught up in a community where people are being made whole, healed bit by bit of the ravages of sin upon their lives; and where relationships are being restored as people from different classes, backgrounds and cultures come together around the person of Jesus – people who have nothing in common except an awareness that much is wrong in their own lives and in the society around them, and only Jesus can put it right.

But that community is not brought together by God to be inward-looking and to concentrate only on making itself whole and holy. That community is brought together by God to be both a model and a launchpad: a model of how people can live together in today's fragmented world, and a launchpad that blasts people out into that world with a message of wholeness and restoration at the personal and social level. Church is where we learn to live with each other despite our differences. It is the community through which we learn that diversity is a good thing; God does not want us all to be the same, otherwise he wouldn't have made us all so wonderfully different. God wants us to take those lessons into our work-places, our social clubs, our community groups and tenants' associations – even our political parties. And God wants us to be rooted in church as the place where we find strength and support, encouragement and teaching as we seek to live out the lessons in the wider world.

Dave Andrews is an Australian Christian who works in a poor area of Brisbane, building community among the dispos-sessed. In his book *Building a Better World*, he wrestles with what it means to be a community and how we can achieve it with all our imperfections. It is a stimulating and richly rewarding read. He describes his concept of community as involving the following things: 'It is a safe place; there is accep-tance of people as part of a group; there is respect for the unity and diversity of people in the group; every person participates in the decisions of the group; and there is support for processes that do justice to the most disadvantaged – not only those inside but also those outside the group.'[11] It seems to me that this is a pretty good description of church – or at least of what church should be striving to be.

But more important than that, it seems to me that if church can be these things, it gives us a launchpad and a model to seek to create these things, with other people of goodwill, in the communities, towns and cities in which we live. In other words, church is the vital base from which we get involved with God in his work of getting the values he espouses and stands for into our world. Without church, with all its pain as well as its wonder and beauty, we shall not be able to achieve these things in the wider world – the things that are to do with God's kingdom; the things Jesus died to make a reality; the things the Holy Spirit inspires in his people; the things, in short, that the church was born to model.

Through our commitment, critical belonging and creative participation, we can help the church to live up to this high calling. Without us, the church will struggle to be what God wants it to be, because he wants every Christian fully involved with his project to redeem the planet. And that means working in and with and through the church.

So get stuck in!

Conclusion

Does the future have a church?

I was talking to mate and mission adviser Darrell Jackson about the church and the theme of this book. 'Ah,' he said. 'Does the future have a church?' And I thought that that question helpfully brings things to a conclusion.

We've looked at the trouble the church in the UK is in. We've pored over statistics that make for gloomy reading and we've shared stories of how church has done harm to individuals and been a difficult place to be. We've tried to measure the depth of the hole the church has fallen into. And, on the positive side, we've looked at what the New Testament says about the church and how this might work itself out in practice, albeit imperfectly, in situations where people were willing to give it a go. Finally, we've asked how we might maximize the benefits and minimize the harm – to us and to the congregation – of our involvement in church.

So, it just leaves us with this final question: does the future have a church? We'll all have to bring our own answer to this, from our own reading of Scripture, the world around us and, of course, from our experience of church. After all we've talked about in this book, I still believe that the answer is a qualified 'Yes'.

In his usual provocative way, Mike Riddell puts his finger on the key issue when he says, 'The church in the West is a terminal case, strapped down on a stainless-steel slab and in desperate need of attention. But, unlike those who pray so passionately, I'm not keen for her to get up and walk in her present form ... My own prophecy, by which I stand or fall, is that without significant reformation (read "surgery") the Western church is headed for the knacker's yard.'[1]

I actually see three signs of hope that might suggest that the surgery needed for the church in the UK may be starting to happen.

Seeking the welfare of the city

The first is that the church is doing things and people are noticing. Whether it's Peggy going to her lunch club or Chris to his day centre, Jack finding help with his debts or Melanie getting job training, lots of people are going to church these days and getting exactly the help and support they're looking for. This might sound like an odd place to begin, but churches that get involved in such social ministries are putting themselves on the map in a new and significant way. They are also having to ask themselves far-reaching questions about their attitudes to outsiders, their purpose for being in the communities they find themselves in, and, most fundamentally, what the good news of Jesus has to say not only about souls but also about society.

In fact, over the past decade many have come to see 'the church' as a key source of thinking about and provision of social welfare and support for needy people and communities. The think-tank Demos produced a widely read and hugely influential report at the back-end of the 1990s examining the persistence of faiths in an allegedly secular Britain. It reported: 'Much of the best innovation in the provision of local health, homelessness, community regeneration and drug-related services are now being shaped by people with strong religious beliefs.'[2]

Evidence of this can be seen all over the UK where churches are establishing projects to reach out to needy groups in their communities. From Oasis Trust to Pecan, the M13 Youth Project in Manchester to Bethany Christian Trust in Edinburgh, there are tons of excellent projects not only providing tangible help but also speaking prophetically to our society about the needs of the poor and the excluded.[3] We noted earlier that many churches are the only functioning voluntary-sector body in their areas, and this is increasingly noticed by government. All the major political parties want to engage with faith-based communities – the overwhelming majority of which are Christian – in order to see if welfare can be delivered more effectively in partnership with them. This makes churches very visible in their communities and leads to people finding faith in Christ (as we saw in chapters 3 and 4).

To engage effectively in social action – especially large-scale projects of the kind mentioned above – requires a relatively large and formally organized church or a number of churches working in partnership. But it is not impossible for a small, informal church, cell or neighbourhood group to engage in significant small-scale social action. For example, a cell group near a care home for adults with learning difficulties decided to invite small numbers of residents to a member's home for tea on Sunday afternoons. This simple idea enabled Christians to get to know a group they wouldn't normally have had any contact with, and gave the residents of the care home the chance to get out, make new friends and feel more independent than they had done.

Larger-scale social-action projects could point to a longer-term future for more traditionally organized churches than the statistics might suggest. However, such churches will have to think quite radically about their theology and how they can involve the maximum number of their people in thinking about such services as well as delivering them.

Many people who have struggled with church have found a role for themselves within a Christian congregation through helping to organize and deliver some kind of local social ministry. Here is one place that fruitful dialogue between a struggling church and Christians struggling to find a place within it can reap great benefits for both parties – and for people beyond the doors of the church.

The second sign of hope is the emergence of a number of new-style churches. These function as working models of new ways of doing church. Lots of people these days are talking about the 'emerging church' as something new, appearing here and there on the ecclesiastical landscape. Reports of such initiatives are beginning to appear in print[4] and resources for them are being posted on the web.[5]

So, for example, a small group of people meet at Rod's house on Tuesday evenings. They share a meal, talk about their jobs and then read the Bible together, pray and go home. None is involved in a more formal church but all are committed to maintaining their life and witness as Christians in demanding jobs.

The thing that makes me most hopeful about such models is that very few of them require huge numbers or vast resources to bring them about. All they need is thought and determination on the part of a small group of Christians committed to doing something to address the deficiencies in their own experience of church, which might lead to others who struggle finding a place of belonging among them. And none requires that the old ways of doing church be abandoned before the new way can emerge. In many cases, emerging models of church are working side by side with existing churches and are supported by them.

This again suggests that ministers struggling to find ways of making church relevant to those who don't see the point and don't get involved could have extremely fruitful dialogue with them over new, different and sometimes radical ways of doing church. Such experiments could exist alongside traditional church and be a way of helping those sceptical about new ways of doing things to see that their positive benefits for the church's mission far outweigh the costs of setting them up. We'll pick this idea up later.

The third sign of hope is the very fact that people are asking questions and wanting to try new things. Every ministers' conference I attend (of which there are many!) and every service I take (some 160 in the past three years, almost all in different churches) offers some opportunity to talk about how we should be doing church in the twenty-first century. More than that, people today seem to be open as never before to new ideas and models from overseas as well as from other parts of the UK.

I believe that if ministers and leaders and those who struggle to find a place in a church can talk to one another about ways of doing church, about how we engage people of all kinds with the good news of Jesus, and about how we do mission in a postmodern culture, great things will happen to the church.

Asking ourselves the hard questions

Does the future have a church? I think that's up to all of us. I said at the outset of our journey that this was not a book of answers but of questions – though I hope that along the way you might have picked up some pointers to where answers might lie. I want to round it off by asking some more direct questions that I hope will help you to decide whether *your* future has a church.

What follows is a kind of checklist for those wanting to deepen and broaden their engagement with church – all the way from people who've recently quit, to those on the cusp of leaving, to those who feel their experience of church is getting stale, tired or boring, to leaders and ministers struggling to create churches that scratch where increasing numbers itch.

Whatever our attitude to church, it is very healthy to think over the involvements we have. Some people, from time to time, audit their careers. (Have I achieved what I set out to do? Am I able to use the skills and talents I have? Is what I do fulfilling?) Perhaps we need to do the same with our church life. Before doing anything about church, therefore, we need to take stock, think, reflect and ponder. Then we need to talk it over with friends, ministers and leaders – sometimes we need to shout and stamp our feet in order to get heard. We need to be prepared to hang in there and work for change. Sometimes, sadly, it'll be right – having done all that – to walk away and, ideally, look elsewhere.

Has anything in this book inspired you to re-engage with your church in a new way? Perhaps you've read something in it and said, 'Yeah – I want to do that,' or 'I think we should give that a go in our church'? If church has become dull, perhaps something you've read here will brighten it up.

I was talking to someone recently who'd returned to his church after a few years away.

'They're still exactly the same,' he lamented. 'People sit in the same places, we sing the same songs and still talk about the same things …'

He's thinking of leaving. I suggested he offer to spice things up a bit, and to share his experiences away from the church. He'd done a photography course and learned something about looking at everyday things in a new way. Perhaps he could provide something visual for his church's worship to help them see the world differently. People are often prepared to try something new now and again, only to find it becomes a habit. It's easy to carp, better to make a difference.

Maybe you're in church regularly but no-one seems to talk to you. Someone told me about friends of hers, stalwarts in their church over many years, who had begun to feel restless.

'The problem is that no-one really speaks to them apart from the same handful of people each week,' she said.

'Why not encourage them to take the initiative, and invite some people round for a meal?' I suggested.

In order to get something out of church, we often have to put something in. If we sow a seed, we stand more chance of reaping a harvest.

One way of doing this is by trying to get to know people in church in a different context. And a good way of doing that is to find someone you don't know very well who shares an interest of yours. Maybe they're in the same line of work, like the same kind of films, share your love of twitching, whatever. I got to know quite a few people in my church through a shared love of various kinds of music. We swapped stories, albums, news of upcoming gigs and the like. We found it was better to do this around the meal table or in the pub. We even ended up going to gigs together. And, of course, we found ourselves talking about much more, including our life with God and struggles with church. We even pray together.

Maybe you feel an outsider in your church. You remember Mary? No-one spoke to her for months when she started attending her church. She hung in, largely because no one told her not to come! There are two types of outsider in our churches. The first is the newcomer. Most of the onus here is on stalwarts of the church to make the first move, but if you are new in your church and feel able to do so, why not sidle up to someone and say, 'Hello, my name's So-and-so. I'm new here. What's happening?' and see what kind of reaction you get. Nine times of ten it will at least be polite.

A second kind of outsider is the one who's been attending a church for some time, possibly even for years, and feels a growing sense of not belonging. Perhaps the church has moved in a different direction from you. Perhaps new people have come and changed the way it feels. Whatever's happened, your church doesn't feel like 'home' as much as it used to. What to do?

First, don't ask yourself, 'If I was newcomer, would I want to join this church?' Rather ask, 'What's God up to here? Do I want to be part of it?' Then talk to your friends. Find out if they feel the same. Talk to your minister or a leader.

Gladys doesn't like drama, new music or casual clothes. But she was one of my most trusted deacons when I first started out as a pastor. In many ways she felt like an outsider at the church she worshipped in, and yet was prepared to acknowledge that God was doing things, people were being reached with the good news and the church was growing. She was an asset to me because she asked uncomfortable questions about what I was doing and why. But she supported what we were doing, even though she didn't like some of it, because she recognized that God was doing stuff in our midst. Fancy being a Gladys in your church? It isn't easy, but it is rewarding for all concerned.

Trapped in an exclusion zone?

Maybe you feel excluded from your church. You come along and people are friendly enough, but no-one seems interested in what contribution you could make, or in what your gifts are. Why not look at the church's programme and ask yourself if there's anywhere in it where your gifts could be used. Then talk to the leaders and see what happens.

Perhaps you've got gifts, skills and interests that the church isn't using but ought to be. I heard a wonderful story recently about two six-year-olds picked up by the police because they were wandering the streets of their town. The officers stuck the kids in their car and said, 'We'll take you home.'

'We want to go to the church,' the kids responded. 'They take care of us there.'

What a great picture of church that is! But it wouldn't have been true of this one had a couple not gone to their minister and said, 'We must do something for the kids who hang around our church on Sunday morning.'

This church, a small struggling concern on a difficult estate, had initially said that it really didn't have the resources to mount any kind of children's work. The couple persisted, saying they had the relevant gifts and experience – plus they felt God was in it. The church caught their vision and enthusiasm, and now, after the morning service on a Sunday, they run a kids' church that is having a far-reaching effect on many young lives – and their families – on the estate. All because a couple said, 'These are our gifts. Please let us use them here.'

Again, this isn't easy, but getting everyone's gifts working in a church is two-way process. Leaders can't be expected to know what everyone in a church could do if unleashed – though perhaps they could do more to find out (as we'll see in a minute). So we sometimes need to take the initiative and push ourselves forward, offer the skills, gifts, talents and time we have and start a conversation with the leaders over how best we could make a contribution. We might find ourselves pushing at an open door.

Sometimes we are reluctant to do this because we fear rejection; indeed, we might have had our offers of involvement spurned in the past. This can leave us feeling deflated, demotivated, even hurt. But if we believe that God has given us a particular gift and our friends agree, then it's good to hang in and keep the offer open. It's good for us because it deepens our self-awareness and knowledge of God. And it's good for our church because it gives them the chance to change their mind, accept our offer and grow as a result. This can't happen if we walk off in a huff.

Perhaps you have been deeply hurt by something that has happened in church. This is an immensely difficult and sensitive area. If ever there were situations where we need to move slowly and prayerfully, it's here. Nearly always we need to begin by looking at ourselves and seeing whether there are things we should forgive and move on from, things we could have handled better, or things we need to repent of and put behind us. Always we need to involve others in the process. Some hurts can be healed by time and conversation. Others can be dealt with only by surgery.

I hurt friends of mine who were youth workers in a church where I was a leader. The leadership had made a decision and assumed that the youth groups would go along with it. My friends were very upset. They talked of standing down, even of leaving the church. As a leadership we apologized, abandoned the course of action we'd decided on, and consulted. Relationships were restored and we'd learned a better way of doing things.

When Don's marriage collapsed, his church grew cool towards him. It wasn't his fault. His wife had left him for another man. But relationships were strained. Some years later, he started seeing Penny and they talked of marriage. Don's church talked of barring him from communion. The gloves came off. All Don's pent-up hurt and anger at the way his former friends had treated him came out. Things were said by both sides that, with hindsight, everyone regrets. But there was no going back. He and Penny left the church, married and joined another one.

In both these situations there came the moment when people had to forgive and move on. That isn't easy. But the alternative is to allow the hurt to eat us up, and that risks leaving us bitter and isolated. Pain can be a point of growth in our own lives and in our relationships with others. Are we prepared to use our hurts as a springboard to deeper involvement with people?

Leaders in dialogue

What about leaders? If the future has a church, what do leaders have to do? Here's a checklist for you – one with far-reaching implications.

1. Listen to people who are struggling with church.
2. Allow others to play a part in setting the agenda for teaching.
3. Involve people of all kinds in everything the church does.
4. Decentralize the church's activities.

Let's look at these ideas in more detail.

First, talk with and listen to people struggling with church, even your church. You may like things just the way they are. So might your fellow leaders and even the bulk of the congregation. You may see no reason at all to struggle with it. Often, though, we have blind spots. We like it as it is because we can control it. It's predictable and manageable. The danger is that we slip into a rut and do church for ourselves, according to our gifts and tastes, and those of the people who tell us how good it is. But such a church might actually be drifting away from people on its edge, and be completely invisible to those outside. We need to listen to those who struggle with church as it currently is, in order to stay sharp and focused – especially on those on the fringes and beyond. After all, the church is for them, *more* than it is for you.

In a remarkable book from New Zealand, Alan Jamieson tells how he spoke to people who left church and to the leaders of some of the churches they left. What the leaders told him borders on the scary for the future of the church everywhere. Almost all of them had failed to grasp why anyone would leave their church. They blamed them for not fitting in, even suggesting that some were never really Christians in the first place – despite the fact that many of them had held significant leadership positions in their churches. What comes out clearly from the research is that none of the leaders ever really talked to people who were struggling with the church about the reasons for their dissatisfaction. They assumed everything was OK with their church, and any problem was with the struggling member.[6]

This means, secondly, that we need not only to listen, but also to allow others in our churches to set the agenda for what we do. People who are struggling need to be encouraged to articulate their concerns, so that those who are leading and teaching can seek to address them through the teaching programme of the church. Indeed, why not adopt dialogue models of teaching that encourage people to ask questions and even to raise issues for you to tackle in your teaching ministry? What better than to scratch where people are itching?

In our evening services I followed the rule Oliver Cromwell laid down for regimental chaplains in his New Model Army during the English Civil War. He said that chaplains could preach for as long as they liked, provided they were prepared to be questioned for same length of time by their congregations afterwards. This is an excellent model. It makes us directly accountable for our words and their implications. I found that being asked questions made me prepare better. Also, over time, I altered the focus of what I was doing so that it more directly helped the people in my church to grow in their Christian lives at home, at work and in the world.

Another way we enabled people to have their say was by establishing a teaching team which met to draw up the teaching agenda for the church for the next few months. This team consisted of people who preached in our services. The team approach meant that a variety of concerns was reflected in what we taught on Sunday mornings. I wish I'd brought people who didn't preach into that group, so that their concerns also could have been articulated. Preachers tend to preach on things they know about and find interesting, not necessarily on what their non-preaching listeners are dying to hear about.

Is everyone on board?

Thirdly, leaders must make a conscious effort to involve the maximum number of people in everything they do as a

...urch. 'Oh, if only that were possible!' cries the over-stretched pastor who has yet again failed to fill a vacancy in the Sunday school. I hear that. But it's not really what I have in mind.

Too often we want to fill vacancies in *our* programme and on *our* terms. We've already thought about the story of the church whose agenda was moved on by a couple whose gifts lay in children's work. How open are we as pastors and leaders to hearing God speak in that way? This isn't just a case of filling vacancies. It's about being prepared to axe certain things because God has provided the gifts for other things to happen instead.

But it runs deeper than that. It's also about allowing people of all kinds a shot at involvement in the whole life of the church. The leader of a major Christian charity working with the disabled was sitting next to the leader of a church she was visiting. The service got underway. One of the people taking part was severely disabled. Though able to speak quite clearly, his body was twisted and prone to spasm as he stood on the platform. The leader turned to the visitor and said, 'Oh dear! We mustn't let this happen again. It makes entirely the wrong impression.'

Crass as this comment undoubtedly was, it's a symptom of something all leaders are prone to. We want our public events run by people who'll do a good professional job – in short, who'll do it as we would. I remember being taken to task by Marian, one of the people in my church who leads worship, over who could read and lead prayer in services. I have to admit that I like to hear the Scriptures read well, and I like public intercessions to be well constructed. In our church we had lots of willing people whose public reading and praying made me wince. When I mentioned this at a meeting of worship leaders, Marian accused me of wanting everything to be too professional. She said that I was in danger of limiting involvement in our services to the few who could speak well.

Doing that would exclude the majority of people from involvement on the platform on Sunday mornings. I only half-listened to her, and over time the pool of people willing to take part in our services dropped to those who did it like me. It took a long time to recover the situation. I wish I'd listened to Marian. Our gatherings are not about being crisp and polished. They are about helping one another to meet God.

Finally, consider decentralizing your church's programme. Churches in the West revolve around what happens on Sundays – especially Sunday morning. We judge people's involvement and commitment almost exclusively on the basis of who's there on Sunday morning. We see them as the committed ones, the pool from which we fish for leaders of all kinds. But what about those with a passion for Jesus but who hate the current menu of happy-clappy songs? What about those whose shift patterns don't allow them to get to church more than one Sunday in four (and who often feel like outsiders as a result)? What about those who are involved in local government, or a particularly demanding job, and need a group of Christians to help them thrash out a Christian response to specific tough issues?

The answer might be to try and create a more diffuse community, made up of people of all kinds, meeting at various times and in different places through the week; a community that is resourced with teaching and theology in a variety of ways at a variety of times. This liberates the minister to do the work he or she ought to have been trained for. It could also enable those who are struggling to connect with church to feel that they are part of something that seeks to take their concerns and needs seriously, while at the same time calling them to be accountable to others for their life in Christ. It will also, almost certainly, open up new mission opportunities for the church in your locality.

As I was writing this, I fell into a conversation with a leader in a national Christian youth organization who told me that he'd stopped going to church on Sunday mornings. He meets instead with a group of friends on Sunday evenings. Sometimes they worship formally, sometimes they share a meal, sometimes they chat. He talks of finding a depth of relationship with these people that he'd never encountered in regular church. But the group is still in touch with the church they all met at. The minister is involved in working out the kinds of thing the Sunday-evening group will focus their thinking and worship on. They feel accountable to the church's leadership for the way they do things. But they have no involvement on Sunday mornings – indeed, they turn it down when offered. Some in the church, who were initially hostile to the group, now recognize that it is as much a part of the church as they are. And they see people being introduced to Jesus through this much less formal network who would never have darkened the doors of a more formally structured church. The fact that they don't gather on Sunday mornings doesn't make any difference.

Cell church might be one way of achieving a wider appeal, with different cells having different agendas and emphases and thus attracting different kinds of people all organically linked to one another through joint activities. Such get-togethers ought to be of the 'lowest common denominator' type, such as picnics in the park, or fun days with activities for all ages including children, rather than celebratory worship events (as such things appeal only to a minority).

Another way is through allowing interest groups or affinity groups to form around people, and for the minister to help to resource them theologically, while also giving them space at worship services and church meetings to report from time to time on what they are doing. This way, people get the specific help and support they need in their jobs, community involvement or political life, while at the same time being accountable to and nourished by the wider church family. It means that their commitment to the church is not being measured by attendance on a Sunday. Rather, the church's commitment to them is measured by its willingness to support them in their various callings in the world. As we saw in chapter 2, this is a vital part of what the New Testament says about what church is for.

This list of ideas is by no means complete. But if nothing else, I hope it encourages you to look at your church, to think about it, to talk to people about it, and to thrash out what drives you up the wall about it and what you'd die to keep in it. Above all, I hope it encourages you to decide that the future does have a church, because *your* future has one.

Notes

Introduction: Will the last person to leave church please turn off the lights?

1. Mike Riddell, *Threshold of the Future* (London: SPCK, 1998), p. 1.
2. Ibid., p. 3. The figures, from David Barrett, *World Christian Encyclopaedia* (Nairobi: Oxford University Press, 1982) are twenty years old – if anything, the rate of departure is higher now.
3. Peter Brierley, *The Tide is Running Out* (London: Christian Research, 2000), p. 99.
4. Philip Richter and Leslie Francis, *Gone but not Forgotten: Church Leaving and Returning* (London: Darton, Longman and Todd, 1998).
5. *Christianity*, April 1998, p. 5.
6. Richter and Francis, *Gone but not Forgotten*, p. 146.
7. Ibid., p. 147.
8. Steve Turner, *Imagine* (Leicester: IVP, 2001), pp. 23–24.
9. Callum Brown, *The Death of Christian Britain* (London: Routledge, 2000), p. 2.

1. Stop the church, I want to get off

1. Douglas Kennedy, *In God's Country: Travels in the Bible Belt, USA* (London: Abacus, 1996), p. 96.
2. Philip Richter and Leslie Francis, *Gone but not Forgotten: Church Leaving and Returning* (London: Darton, Longman and Todd, 1998), p. 68.
3. Ibid., p. 69.
4. See Steve Turner's discussion of U2 in *Imagine* (London: IVP, 2001), chapter 8.
5. Bill Flanagan, *U2 at the End of the World* (London: Bantam, 1995), p. 397.
6. Ibid., p. 285.
7. Kennedy, *In God's Country*, p. 107.
8. Morris Stuart, *So Long, Farewell and Thanks for the Church* (Milton Keynes: Scripture Union, 1992), p. 13.
9. Ibid., p. 14.
10. Kennedy, *In God's Country*, p. 105.

2. Yes, but what is it for?

1. I. Howard Marshall, 'How far did the early Christians worship God?', *Churchman* 99 (1985), pp. 216–229.
2. Ibid., p. 220.
3. Robert Banks, *Paul's Idea of Community: The Early House Churches in their Cultural Setting*, revised edition (Peabody, MA: Hendrickson, 1994), p. 88.
4. See my *Discovering the New Testament* (Leicester: Crossway, 2001) chapter 22, for a fuller explanation of this.
5. Banks, *Paul's Idea of Community*, p. 90.
6. Marshall, 'How far did the early Christians worship God?', p. 227.
7. www.barna.org.
8. John Drane, *The McDonaldization of the Church: Spirituality, Creativity and the Future of the Church* (London: Darton, Longman and Todd, 2000), p. 158.

9. Ibid., p. 161.

10. There are lots of resources to help you explore this area further. Two of the best are Brian and Kevin Draper, *Refreshing Worship* (Oxford: Bible Reading Fellowship, 2000), and Mike Riddell, Mark Pierson and Cathy Kirkpatrick, *The Prodigal Project: Journey into the Emerging Church* (London: SPCK, 2000); this comes with a CD ROM containing a directory of alternative-worship projects around the world. If there's one near you, why not go along and check it out?

11. For a fuller explanation of this see my *Discovering Luke's Gospel* (Leicester: Crossway, 1999), especially pp. 181–185.

3. Bringing the church into focus

1. See my *Discovering the New Testament* (Leicester: Crossway, 2001), chapter 4.

2. See ibid., chapters 4 and 10.

4. Somewhere to call home

1. Bill Flanagan, *U2 at the End of the World* (London: Bantam, 1995), p. 96.

2. Ibid., p. 97.

3. Ibid.

4. Ibid.

5. John Ortberg, *Christianity Today*, 19 May 1997.

6. See my *Discovering Luke's Gospel* (Leicester: Crossway, 1999), pp. 85–105, for details.

7. See especially Stephen Cottrell, *Sacrament, Wholeness and Evangelism: A Catholic Approach* (Nottingham: Grove Evangelism Series 33, 1996).

8. Interview in *Christianity*, July 1997, p. 41.

9. Robert and Julia Banks, *The Church Comes Home: A New Base for Community and Mission* (Sutherland, New South Wales: Albatross, 1986); Howard Snyder, *Radical Renewal: The Problem of Wineskins Today* (Houston: Touch

Publications, 1996; original edition, Downers Grove: IVP, 1975); David Prior, *The Church in the Home* (Basingstoke: Marshall Pickering, 1983).

10. Howard Snyder, *The Radical Wesley and Patterns for Church Renewal* (Downers Grove: IVP, 1980).

11. Robert Banks, *Paul's Idea of Community: The Early House Churches in their Cultural Setting*, revised edition (Peabody, MA: Hendrickson, 1994).

5. Me in my small corner

1. The best introduction to postmodernism is still David Lyon, *Postmodernity* (Buckingham: Open University Press, 1994). And the best Christian reflection on it is J. Richard Middleton and Brian J. Walsh, *Truth is Stranger Than it Used to Be: Biblical Faith in a Postmodern Age* (London: SPCK, 1995).

2. Michael Griffiths, *Cinderella with Amnesia: A Practical Discussion of the Relevance of the Church* (London: IVP, 1975), p. 25.

3. Douglas Kennedy, *In God's Country: Travels in the Bible Belt, USA* (London: Abacus, 1996), p. 143.

4. Ibid., pp. 136–137.

5. See my *Discovering Luke's Gospel* (Leicester: Crossway, 1999), pp. 103–105, 109–112.

6. Alan Storkey, 'What is there to celebrate in today's families?', *Church of England Newspaper*, 9 June 1995, p. 9.

6. You'll never walk alone

1. For resources to help you develop the art of meditating and listening to God through a variety of media see Ken Gire, *Windows of the Soul: Experiencing God in New Ways* (Grand Rapids: Zondervan, 1996).

2. Ron Sider, *Rich Christians in an Age of Hunger*, fourth edition (London: Hodder and Stoughton, 1997), chapter 10.

7. Will rearranging the deckchairs be sufficient?

1. Mike Riddell, Mark Pierson and Cathy Kirkpatrick, *The Prodigal Project: Journey into the Emerging Church* (London: SPCK, 2000), p. 18.
2. Philip Richter and Leslie Francis, *Gone but not Forgotten: Church Leaving and Returning* (London: Darton, Longman and Todd, 1998), p. 148.
3. Ibid., pp. 148–149.
4. Dave Tomlinson, *The Post-Evangelical* (London: Triangle, 1995), pp. 82–83.
5. Mark Ireland, *A Study of the Effectiveness of Process Evangelism Courses in the Diocese of Lichfield with Special Reference to Alpha* (undated Sheffield University MA thesis), p. 66. Available from the Lichfield Diocese website at www.lichfield.anglican.org.
6. Callum Brown, *The Death of Christian Britain* (London: Routledge, 2000), p. 6.
7. Ibid., p. 172.
8. Ibid., p. 1.
9. Ibid., p. 239.
10. Barry Linney, *21st Century Faith: Radical Mission in a New Millennium* (London: Marshall Pickering, 2000), p. 3.
11. For examples see Alan Kreider, *Worship and Evangelism in Pre-Christendom*, Joint Liturgical Studies 32 (Cambridge: Grove Books, 1995), p. 20. For a stimulating discussion of Christian social action over the past 200 years see David Smith, *Transforming the World? The Social Impact of British Evangelicalism* (Carlisle: Paternoster, 1998).
12. See Fran Becket et al., *Rebuild: Small Groups Can Make a Difference* (Leicester: Crossway, 2001).
13. Michael Green, *Evangelism through the Local Church* (London: Hodder and Stoughton, 1990), p. ix.
14. David Edwards, quoted in Peter Brierley, *The Tide is Running Out* (London: Christian Research, 2000), p. 30.

15. Riddell, Pierson and Kirkpatrick, *The Prodigal Project*: p. 11.

8. Subverting the church for good

1. Carl Trueman, 'Editorial: Tell it not in Gath', *Themelios* 26.2, spring 2001, p. 3.
2. Ibid., p. 2.
3. Ibid.
4 *Christianity,* July 1997, pp. 38–39.
5. Phil Hill, *The Church of the Third Millennium* (Carlisle: Paternoster, 1999), p. 66.
6. Ibid., pp. 96–102.
7. *The Times*, 17 March 2001, p. 10.
8. Mark Ireland, *A Study of the Effectiveness of Process Evangelism Courses in the Diocese of Lichfield with Special Reference to Alpha* (undated Sheffield University MA thesis), p. 79. Available from the Lichfield Diocese website at www.lichfield.anglican.org.
9. See Mike Riddell, Mark Pierson and Cathy Kirkpatrick, *The Prodigal Project: Journey into the Emerging Church* (London: SPCK, 2000), for ideas.
10. *The Times*, 17 March 2001, p. 10.
11 Dave Andrews, *Building a Better World* (Sutherland, New South Wales: Lancer, 1996), p. 57.

Conclusion: Does the future have a church?

1. Mike Riddell, 'If the church isn't quick, she's dead …', *Third Way*, February 1998, p. 35.
2. 'Keeping the faiths: The new covenant between religious belief and secular power', *Demos Quarterly* 11, May 1997, p. 3.
3. For a study of a wide range of different types of projects being done by churches all over the UK see Fred Catherwood, *It Can Be Done* (Cambridge: Lutterworth

Press, 2000) and Steve Chalke, *Faith Works* (Eastbourne: Kingsway, 2001).

4. See Stuart Murray and Anne Wilkinson-Hayes, *Hope from the Margins: New Ways of Being Church*, Evangelism series 49 (Cambridge: Grove Books, 2000), and Mike Riddell, Mark Pierson and Cathy Kirkpatrick, *The Prodigal Project: Journey into the Emerging Church* (London: SPCK, 2000), for lots of ideas.

5. The following websites are good places to begin: www.tribalgathering.com; www.osbd.org and www.newway.org.uk.

6. Alan Jamieson, *A Churchless Faith: Faith Journeys Beyond Evangelical, Pentecostal and Charismatic Churches* (Wellington, New Zealand: Philip Garside Publishing, 2000) especially chapter 3.